NIGHT FISHING
FOR TROUT

The Final Frontier

NIGHT FISHING FOR TROUT

Revised and Expanded Edition

By JIM BASHLINE

Illustrations By ELDRIDGE HARDIE

Delta

A Delta Book
Published by
Dell Publishing
a division of
Bantam Doubleday Dell Publishing Group, Inc.
666 Fifth Avenue
New York, New York 10103

The trademark Delta® is registered in the U.S. Patent and Trademark
Office.

ISBN: 0-385-30093-X

Reprinted by arrangement with Willow Creek Press

Manufactured in the United States of America

Published simultaneously in Canada

April 1992

10 9 8 7 6 5 4 3 2 1

RRH

CONTENTS

INTRODUCTION TO THE FIRST EDITION

There is something special about every trout stream worthy of being called trout water. It is a fact that all such waters harbor some big nocturnal-feeding fish.

There is something special, too, about the hard-fished sections of a stream, particularly those in densely populated areas where privacy can usually be enjoyed only by the one who goes forth or stays out after the others come in. When these two factors are combined, the result is solitude in conjunction with night-fishing for big trout. This is a pursuit for which some are geared and for which others are in neutral. There are many fly fishermen for trout who know nothing about this game; therefore, until such time as they are exposed to it, they know not whether they are in gear or out of gear with it.

This clever and authoritative book will be an introduction for the novice, an entertainment for the expert, and a source of instruction for both.

Big, husky Jim Bashline is precisely the right man to produce a book on this subject, and this is precisely the right time for such a book to become available. The author was born and raised in the wildest part of Penn's Woods, that high, forested big country that tapers in three directions into three vast watersheds, those of the Allegheny and Genesee Rivers and Pine Creek. All three, in their headwaters, are fine, clean trout streams. One sees cars with bumper stickers that read "Potter County, God's Country." This is the Bashline home country. It is where the bear harvest is the greatest in the East, where there are some grouse that are never flushed by the hunter, and where each mountain stream has its own native population of brook trout, including some big holdovers under dense cover.

In spite of the numbers of fishermen that flock to our streams, certain big fish are never shown a fly or a bait. These are the shy, old trout that reside by day under rocks, roots, banks, and brushpiles, where they contentedly slumber, away from the wares of the daytime angler. At night it is different. They let down their guard and come into the open to feed. It is then only that they may encounter something on the business end of a rod and line.

Jim Bashline was born in the right place, and just in time to be well schooled. He learned the art of night fishing from the pioneers and foremost proponents of the game, at the foremost spot in the land for the practice of it. But the story of the Goodsell Hole is for Jim to tell.

This book covers patterns, places, practices, and people, but most important, it covers fish and fishing. I know that Jim knows a great deal about night fishing and that he is highly skilled at it, because I have heard him talk on the subject and have watched him perform. Every so often he shows up at my place about dusk and informs me that, "we are going after them tonight." It is because of these escapades and because of his knowledge, enthusiasm, and writing talents that I am delighted that he has seen fit to contribute this much-needed volume to our marvelous array of old and new trout-fishing titles.

Charles K. Fox
Letort Meadows
July, 1972

JUSTIFICATION

I like to fish for trout with flies — for all kinds of trout and with all kinds of flies. In fact, I enjoy fishing for all kinds of fish, but particularly for trout and especially after dark. If you have an aversion to nighttime operations, turn back now, because most of the episodes and observations chronicled herein have a black-shrouded setting. But if you *will* know trout in as many of their aspects as possible, and have yet to cast a fly at night, I think you will be curious. If you have tasted only a nip of night fishing, you will probably be stimulated enough to want to read on. If you are an inveterate after-dark fly man, you must read on, to compare notes, of course.

I did not come to night fishing for trout by design. It was inevitable for me. Tradition in my northcentral Pennsylvania homeland decreed that any angler worth the name would fish after dark. Local conditions, combined with the introduction of the brown trout, made night fishing the quickest way to taking a fish that couldn't be made to lie straight in the creel. During my formative fishing years (a period that is still going on) I at one time thought that the frequent willingness of large browns to strike at night was a peculiarity of the streams I

13

knew best. Trips to more exotic waters have convinced me that this is not so. (To me, exotic waters are any stream that I have never fished before.)

For reasons that I won't attempt to explain, I have never graduated beyond what E.R. Hewitt described as the second stage of an angler's development, that stage being the one in which the angler craves to catch the biggest trout possible. In the first stage, of course, he wants to catch the most trout possible, and the last stage, naturally, has something to do with catching the smartest trout possible. My guess is that most of us are in the second stage, and it could be questioned whether there should be a third stage. After all, the really big river cruisers get that way because they are smart. No, I'm not suggesting that trout possess any capacity for reasoning; I certainly don't want to get into that foolishness. But, in time, they do become phenomenally cautious.

If an angler was a bait-dangler before the gospel of the fly fell upon him, the chances are good that he has hung a really big trout or two, and after his salvation he will doubtless still long for another bend of consequence to appear in his rod — second-stager, pure and simple. Those select few who have never lofted a nightcrawler or strung a minnow are usually second-stagers too. They've had their fill of fighting ten-inch trout to a standstill. The big one is their goal. Yes, they have known the broken tippet, the false rise, the huge swirl, the almost, the nearly, many times. In civilized waters, an eighteen-incher is just about the best the daytime caster of flies can hope for. In fact, I can think of very few anglers who wouldn't construct a damn fine story out of the catching of an eighteen-inch trout in any stream in the United States. An occasional two-footer is subdued on a strand of less than 2X, but this is really big-league stuff, guaranteeing a local reputation that won't lose its luster for at least five full years. Jolly good sport, this business of almost catching the big trout on a fly. Oh, an odd kype-nosed brown or potbellied rainbow or brookie will fall to a streamer now and then, when all conditions are just so, but if the man who fishes hard-fished public waters and prefers to fish with flies wants to number his lifetime catch of trophy fish on a tally sheet instead of on one hand, he should consider night fishing.

Not sporting, you say? This argument really snarls my fur. Trout are frequently just as selective at night as they are by day. A sloppy cast at the tail-end slick of a pool can spook them just as quickly at midnight as it will at high noon. And if you want to release your trout unharmed, the somewhat heavier tackle used in night fishing will enable you to fight him to a quick finish, and he'll swim away with a flash instead of the off-center wobble he'd have had after being fondled nearly to death by the tender touch required by multi-X leaders. I hasten to say that casting the 6X or 7X tippets with the Jassid and other invisiblia is dandy fun if you want to raise some good fish in special locations. But it takes a delicate hand to land even a fourteen-incher on this kind of gear; to beach an eighteen-inch fish on 6X is an outstanding achievement. A two-footer on the same tippet could only be compared with some of the occurrences in the Old Testament. On the famous Letort I once succeeded in finally subduing a twenty-one-inch fish on a 6X leader, and it was fun. But — and the Letort regulars would sneer at me for saying this — I'd have enjoyed the battle and the catch much more if I'd taken the same fish on a size-6 Governor at 2:00 a.m. My guess is that the strike would have been more exciting, the battle more splash-filled and — well, night fishing gets into your blood. It has prejudiced my thinking, I suppose.

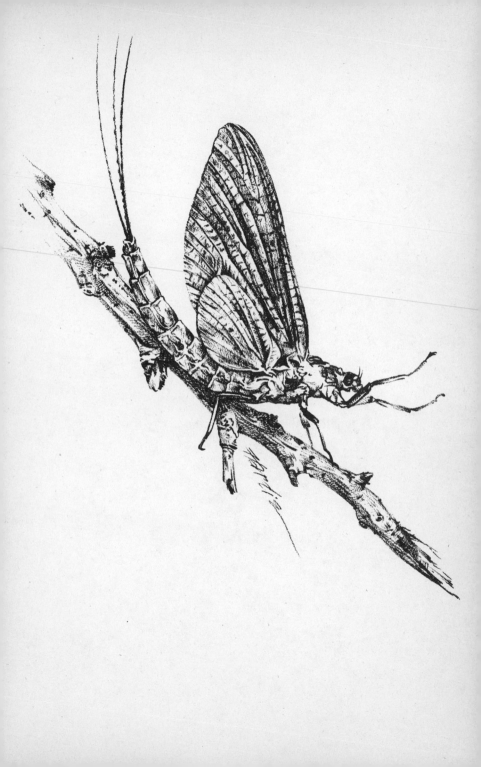

MOTIVATION

During the early weeks of a given trout season, most really good hatches terminate as darkness settles in. Air and water temperature are probably the dominant factors that curtail the emerging insects. The trout stop feeding heavily because food in quantity is no longer present. As the rise tapers off, most fly fishermen reel up and call it a day. At some undefined hour during the middle part of the season, though, air and water temperatures reach an optimum balance and flies will continue to hatch, causing the trout to feed on into the dark hours. In most trout-fishing country, when the daytime temperatures start averaging slightly over 80 degrees and the corresponding water temperatures begin to hit 70 degrees, the evening rise starts later and sometimes may not start at all. But it is very likely that there will be a feeding session at some time during the twenty-four-hour period. The chances are much better than even that various causes, such as large numbers of fishermen (especially in the hard-fished East), will add to the trout's inclination to feed after dark.

It may come as a surprise to some daylight-only fishermen, but there are many mayflies that are predominantly nocturnal hatchers. Under certain conditions, the big Green Drake (*Ephemera guttulata*) will appear in great numbers after dark. On eastern waters the beginning of this hatch usually marks the start of the night-fly season. Many of the large *Hexagenias* are night fliers, and so is the beautiful *Potomanthus distinctus*. Add to these the myriad moths, stone flies, June bugs, and miscellaneous creatures that plague the daytime angler after he's hit his porch chair with highball in hand, and it's obvious that there is no shortage of food for the night cruiser to look over.

A fluke happening that offers food after dark will sometimes present an opportunity. On some waters the measuring worm is one of these happenings. I enjoyed an unforgettable session on the Oswayo River one July night just because by luck I happened to have the right fly on at the right time. The fly was a Grizzly King with wings that were practically nonexistent. It so happened that my particular tie had a shade of green on the body that must have appeared to be "measuring-worm green," for the trout couldn't seem to stay away from it. I tried other flies that evening, but the green-bodied one was taken to the exclusion of all others.

Much learned prose has been written concerning the curious nature of the brown and why he should be the darling of the dry-fly devotee. Much ink has been spilled telling all true believers that once a brown trout reaches hook-billed proportions he is no longer a fly fish and should be removed from a good fly stream. One British writer has gone so far as to suggest that gigging should be legal during special seasons and that trout over four pounds should then be harpooned. Of course there's some truth to the nasty stories told about big trout. They do eat their cousins, nephews, and children from time to time, and they don't fall into a frenzy at the prospect of sucking in some microscopic bit of floating feathers. There are some few instances that will disprove this last generality, but consider how many fish over four pounds you have seen that were taken on the dry fly. Big trout become suspicious, solitary, selective, and seldom find their way into creels. But these same large browns will sometimes display a complete character reversal and seize something that ordinarily would scare them half to death. These sudden fits of irrational behavior occur infrequently during daylight hours. They are *fairly common* at night. The brook trout and the rainbow trout share a bit of this nighttime madness, but the brown is the fish that eventually intrigues the would-be night fisherman, and besides, the brookie and the rainbow do plenty of crazy things during the day.

All of us who have fished for trout for more than a few seasons have either experienced or heard about some such story as the following: "The trout weren't coming up to any of my small flies, so for some unknown reason I tied on this big whumpus fly, made one cast, and, well, it was the biggest trout I took all season! He charged right out from under that log like he'd been waiting all year for that silly thing. . . . What does it look like? Oh, it's just a bunch of odds and ends from the fly-tying table, wound onto a number-6 hook. I never did intend to fish it," etc., etc. In the variations on this tale, the whumpus fly takes many forms. It may be a bass bug, a huge streamer fly, a number-4 Parmachene Belle fished during the redquill hatch, or even a dead sparrow. (This last occurred at least once. I saw it happen.)

The phenomenon of the selective brown trout coming to an outlandish creation during the daytime, while a good hatch is in progress, contains an important message for the student of "the black art" of night fishing. Invariably, an autopsy preformed on such a "whumpus-caught" fish will reveal a nearly empty stomach. I am suggesting that these fish are night feeders who happened to get carried away during the daylight hours and attempted to destroy some out-of-place creature. I am further suggesting that a large share of the heroicly proportioned trout available in the world today are predominantly night feeders and are seldom available to daytime fishermen. We have already mentioned a few of the environmental reasons why some trout are night feeders. I am convinced that, aside from these factors, certain brown trout will remain night feeders whatever their surroundings. This is, I believe, another means that the magnificent brown has of carrying on his species in the face of considerable adversity.

At a former residence in the Allegheny Mountains a few years back, it was my good luck to have a trout pond ten feet away from the back-porch steps. A small pond, about thirty-five-feet square, it was home for about two dozen Kamloops rainbows. Pretty fish and fast growers, they provided entertainment for both fishing and nonfishing friends. During the second week of June, 1962, my nephew, Doug Frederick, brought a fine seventeen-inch brown as a house guest of the rainbows. A night-caught fish, it had been kept alive during a six-mile drive. How Doug kept the fish in a two-gallon bucket and drove the car at the same time I don't know. We nursed the fish for a time in a larger bucket, gradually adding pond water. We thought that this precaution was necessary because the pond temperature was ten to twelve degrees colder than the brown's previous home. After a few false starts, the trout slowly finned out into the pond. We followed him for a time with a flashlight, and it soon was apparent that he would be all right.

The fish sulked under a rock ledge for four days. He would have no part of the wild slashing that took place when a handful of food pellets were thrown onto the surface. On the fifth day of his captivity, he made a furtive exploration around the pond, and on the sixth he sucked up a couple of pellets that had drifted to the bottom. During the two years that we observed him, not once did we ever see him coming to the surface to feed. Good fly hatches from a nearby stream kept the pond well supplemented with natural protein, and the rainbows took advantage of them. The lone brown may have too, but we're quite sure that he didn't do so during the day. The amusing part of this very unscientific experiment was that during a two-year period I was able to catch and release that fish at least a half dozen times at night. That's fairly conclusive evidence that this fish preferred to dine at a more refined hour than his rainbow roommates.

Any observant fisherman who has lingered on after the stars come out knows that the night air frequently seems to bring a halt to the rise. Time for the daytime fisherman to go home. . . . But wait, what's that? A looping swirl at the tail end of the pool. It certainly didn't look like a typical rise, and it most certainly was not. An eagle-billed night cruiser has dropped a hint that he is there. His prey was probably a minnow or a back-peddling crayfish that hoped to make the lip of the pool before becoming an appetizer. This is the classic night fly-fishing setup — a big fish operating in the slick tail glide of a large pool. Read on, poor underprivileged day fisherman. I'll make a believer out of you yet!

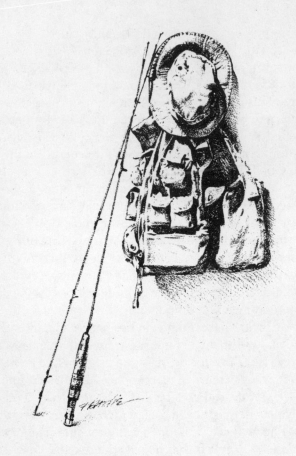

THE RIGHT SETUP

In the shooting-and-hunting game we frequently hear stories about this or that chap who is a fine target shot but does poorly when faced with flesh-and-blood creatures. And of course there's the opposite type of shooter, who regularly each year drills his venison with one running shot but comes completely unglued when faced with a white-and-black piece of paper. I don't believe such a block exists between the daytime fly fisher and his nocturnal counterpart. Forty-four years of day and night fly fishing have made me sure that all forms of tossing the fur-and-feather-adorned hooks tend to improve one's overall ability. To be sure, the fly-fishing basics must be learned during the daylight hours. The casting movements and the automatic responses of the free hand to slack line and reel must become rote before the fisherman can expect to do well at night. The after-dark game offers the angler a chance to hone his reflexes and responses to the subtle signals that he sees and feels at night. Because of his dependence on the touch sense, the accomplished night fisherman is invariably an excellent nympher and, by modifying his technique somewhat, will do well on Atlantic salmon and steelhead.

The daytime man with a few seasons under his belt knows something about where trout are most likely to lie in his favorite streams. This knowledge will serve him well if he decides to sample night fly fishing. He knows that the biggest trout in the pool will have the best hiding place and the best feeding position. With some variations, this same situation prevails at night. Smooth shallow glides that fan out before broken water starts are the classic locations for presenting the dry fly. If the glide happens to flow out of a pool with enough deep water to harbor big trout, you will also have the classic night-fly pool. I'm sure your favorite brown trout stream has such a pool. It's the best place to begin one's night-fly education because all the basics can be learned right there.

The trout are drawn to these pool-end feeding locations because the food is abundantly present there. This is where the dancing spinners lay their eggs, the baitfish congregate, and the current is just right for trout to hold an easy position. However, the trout knows that this is a vulnerable location, and he must be constantly on the alert against predators, among which man is a principal actor.

Standard procedure for the dry-fly man is to attack this location with a quartering cast, usually "lining" any fish that might be there. Even if he doesn't drop line or leader on top of a rising trout, the ever-increasing drag of the current soon puts his fly into high gear, and the job is botched again. There are other ways to deal with trout rising in this location. If a suitable casting location can be found, you could make a downstream parachute cast. If you are a really accomplished caster, you could throw one of those fancy "button-hooks" into the last few feet of line and leader and make your fly hang above the drag for a few seconds longer. Or — you could cast a wet-fly after dark and probably catch your trout.

In this typical night fly setup, it follows that we should use the standard night-fly technique. This consists of casting the fly (flies) slightly upstream and allowing them to drift naturally while keeping excess slack out of the cast by means of the hand-twist retrieve. "Why, hell," says the daytime angler, "that's exactly how I fish wet flies on the ———" (fill in your favorite stream). He's right, of course. This is the most common method of handling the wet fly and has been for a hundred years, at least. It's still one of the best techniques for day and night work. Let's consider it for a moment.

Assume that we've stayed on after dark this night and kept to one position while our eyes adjusted to the darkness. We now detect a rising trout. Because it is early in the night-fly season, I'll suggest that you tie on a Hardy's Favorite as the lead fly and a Lord Baltimore as a dropper, both on size-8 hooks. You make the cast about six feet upstream from where you saw the last rise. As the flies drift over the trout's lie, there is a bulge and a hollow sound that can best be described as a *blup*. There is pressure on your rod hand, you react by striking hard, and there's a sound that the daylight angler who fishes mainly for trout seldom hears — a running reel! Big brown trout usually make a terrific run at night, forty feet or more sometimes, and they invariably turn up with one good jump, sometimes two. Fight him hard! You can afford to because you're rigged up with a tippet of at least four-pound test. You can't see the line, but if you keep the fish on for more than fifteen seconds, you'll probably land him. The night strike is usually a hard one, and the larger hook will have a good grip in his mouth.

IMPLEMENTATION

Nearly every book that deals with fishing has something to say about tackle. There are two reasons for this: It makes the book longer and it gives the author a chance to talk about his favorite rods. Both reasons apply here.

You can fish after dark with any fly rod of between four and sixteen feet, but you will do your best job with a rod somewhere between these two extremes. My personal, special night fly rod is a Leonard "parabolic" that measures seven feet, nine inches. Its length has nothing to do with my liking for it. In fact, I would probably like it even better if it were a bit longer. Its sensitive tip makes it ideal for swimming the large night flies. I have handled some very short rods that would do well for night fishing, but rods of seven feet or more usually do a much better job.

That word *sensitive* is the key term in selecting a good rod for night work. In most cases, you will feel the strike but not see it (although you may hear it), and a very stiff rod does not telegraph the strike as a sensitive one does, and it can't react as well to the movements of a hooked fish. The stiff rod that I'm referring to is the sort that most manufacturers choose to designate as having "dry-fly action." Just why many of them build these rods I'm not sure. They are often so abominably rigid that it takes a WF9 line to make an eight-foot rod begin to flex. Gear like that may be fine for showing off on the lawn when a hundred-foot cast is guaranteed to impress the gallery, but such outfits certainly don't fish very well.

(If I may wander off the path for a moment, I'd like to deliver a light slap at the fishing tackle manufacturers. For many years they have perpetuated the myth that most fly fishermen use a line that is much too light for their rods. There would be some truth to this if all our casts were of sixty feet and beyond, but most of our casts are only about thirty feet and seldom beyond fifty. Regardless of what I've got on the end of my leader, I would much prefer to lay down a DT5F or a DT6F on top of a feeding fish rather than make waves with a WF9 or WF8. The fish are far less likely to head for the nearest cover. My advice is to fish with the lightest line you can possibly handle. You will surely catch more fish, day or night.)

I've been taken to task by some of my fishing friends about this business of using lighter lines for most fly fishing, including some nighttime endeavors. I will back off just a bit, but not much. It is true that beginning fly fishers will do better with a line that flexes the rod in a more pronounced way. For instance, short casts, say not over 30 feet, can be made more easily with a six-weight rod equipped with a seven-weight, double-taper line. This will happen at this range because the heavier line will "shoot" through the guides when less than perfect timing is employed. As one's skill increases, and more distance becomes possible, lighter lines can be delivered. This happens when the "feel" of the tackle and the dynamics of casting a fly rod become automatic instead of being thought about constantly. It's not unlike shooting birds on the wing. When a certain level of proficiency is attained, thinking about the front sight or precisely where the barrels are pointed becomes an insignificant matter. The good wingshooter simply points the shotgun and trusts his reflexes to do the job.

The long, graceful casts that seem to project the line into another solar system (the kind of casts demonstrated by fishing heros on the lawns of motels) are of little practical value when one is night fishing. In fact, such long distance heaving is counterproductive in most situations. The strikes can't be felt on a long line, and fish are not hooked well if at all. With few exceptions, the same can be said for dry-fly fishing. Several feet of slack line hanging beneath the rod tip usually means a delayed strike and a missed fish.

A reasonably good caster can toss a dry fly 35 feet or so with nearly any line on any rod. But that same good caster (or anyone for that matter) will drop the fly in a much softer manner with a five-weight line than he will with an eight weight. This can be compensated for with a longer leader, but when night fishing, a longer leader is out of place. Therefore, most of the time, I'll chose a seven-weight rod tossing a six-weight line as the ideal night outfit. An eight-weight rod throwing a seven-weight line is the number two all-arounder.

The biggest reason night fishermen can get away with lighter lines and still deliver the fly or flies in a decent manner is the weight of the flies themselves. Waterlogged wet flies in suitable night sizes are heavy and help propel the entire terminal rig. But in case you're new to flies larger than a size 12, remember that as the weight of the flies increases, the typical back and forth motions of casting must be slowed down a bit. Instead of the zippy "snap-snap" action of false casting a tiny dry on fifteen feet of line with a ten-foot leader, twenty-five feet of fly line and a six- or eight-foot leader weighs more. Instead of "snap-snap," it's more like "whoosh-whoosh." Come to think of it, that's exactly what three wet flies winging through the night air sound like.

That Leonard I referred to is a model that unfortunately is no longer being manufactured. I suppose I should tuck mine away in a closet and only bring it out to show it off. I won't, though, because it handles so well it would be a shame not to use it. It has that sensitive tip that works so well with night flies and yet has the reserve butt power to skid a sizable fish out onto a gravel bank. And the rod once belonged to Robert N. Pinney, the greatest night fly fisherman I have ever known. You'll hear more about Pinney later.

In spite of their high prices, Leonard rods are still excellent investments. Today the Leonard Company is but a footnote in angling history. But it is quite a footnote to be sure, because, in the minds of many trout and salmon anglers, Leonard split-cane rods were the finest ever built. Some of their trout rods were extremely thin of tip and didn't last long in the hands of stumblebums, but these rods could really perform! I hope that, somehow, the Leonard tapers will be resurrected one day — stranger things have happened — but realistically, those who would know what a Leonard feels like will have to borrow one or buy a used model. A decent second-hand Leonard is currently tagged at over $800, and one in fine condition will cost much more.

It's a convenient trap, this thing of droning on about bamboo rods. Those of us who grew up pouring over the old sporting catalogs can't help getting glaze-eyed when we see an

L.C. Smith Ideal grade 20 gauge or a vintage cane rod. One of these gems in nearly new condition is an exciting find, but finding a classic shotgun or fly rod that wears the proud patina of honest use is like finding a time capsule. It's the narcotic of the blood-sport people who have seen 50 or more calendars become obsolete.

As with fiberglass rods before them, the newer graphite and boron rods are here in spades, and anglers who don't own at least one graphite rod today must be fishing on another planet. There's no need to dip into rod-making archives for a discussion of some of the early graphite rods, however; in a word, they were terrible. With few exceptions the pioneer builders of graphite fly rods did what most pioneers do when fashioning a tool: They made it rugged and functional and left it to others to refine the designs.

The tackle business today, however, is a stellar example of the American style of marketing. "New," "improved," "better," "redesigned," "revolutionary": these marketers' expletives appropriately describe advances in the manufacturing of tackle, and frankly, anglers have been pretty well served by improved technology. We do have some magnificent graphite rods today, and it's difficult to see how they can possibly be made much better.

There is a part of the graphite/boron promotional verbiage that does, however, give me some mild heartburn. It's the strange need some makers have to insist that their rod has "more" graphite in it than other rods do. Such chattering is amalgamated balderdash! I don't care a whit about the percentage of graphite in anybody's rod. The primary concern is how the rod *fishes*. What a rod is made of is of no consequence to the fish and should not be to an angler. I have fished with rods that were advertised to contain 100 percent graphite (an impossibility, by the way) and some that carried less than 15 percent, and found that both fished extremely well.

Several dozen rod makers are supplying us with some great rods today. I have no axe to grind or profit to make from mentioning any particular rod, but there are some which deserve special attention. Considering today's vast line-up of rod makers, trying every fly rod model made would require several lifetimes — and I'd much rather be fishing, so the sticks I'll mention are ones I've spent some time with on the water.

I've long been a Fenwick fan, and during the late 70's that company introduced a series of rods they labeled "Traditional." These were graphite rods with some of the muscle taken out. The idea was to build a graphite rod that more closely resembled bamboo in feel and casting style, meaning not quite so "quick" but still retaining the "telegraphic feel" of graphite. In my opinion, they achieved this, and the eight-foot rod for the six-weight line is one of the finest all around trout rods I've ever seen or used. Fenwick also made an eight-and-a-half-foot rod for the eight-weight line that tosses a seven-weight line with night flies with great style. These rods wore a cigar-shape grip that was reminiscent of many bamboo rods, and that may have been one reason I liked them so much. They had that marvelous "tip-in-hand" feel that is so advantageous when night fishing. The graphite material conducts vibrations better than anything in the world, and yet these rods (particularly the eight-and-a-half-footer for the eight-weight line) make those night flies go *whoosh-whoosh* in a nice, measured cadence as well as any rod I've fished with. But, alas, there was little demand for such a rod, and the only place you'll find these Fenwicks with the "bamboo action" is on the second-hand market or tucked away in the corner of some out-of-the-way tackle store. If you find one, grab it!

The rods made by Sage are among the handsomest of graphites and they perform as well as they look. Unlike some graphite makers, Sage designers softened their sticks' action without losing power in the butt. Their eight-and-a-half-foot rod for the six- and seven-weight line is a fine choice for the night fisherman.

The revered Orvis name is one of the best known in American outdoor circles. While I can't speak with authority about some of their most recent introductions, they turned out a rod some years back that was a minor marvel. It was designted "Presentation" and was nine-and-a-half-feet long. The rod was geared for the eight-weight line, but I used a seven on it most of the time for night fishing. On some waters the length was a bit unhandy, but for twitching flies on the surface, or close to it, the extra length enabled one to do tricks. This rod has a beautiful touch at night, and the tip is soft enough to flex with a hard strike and do most of the hook-setting itself. This rod is, by the way, a fine light salmon rod with an eight-weight line. Seventy foot casts with a long leader and weight-forward line are quite effortless. If that rod is not being made at the time you read this, and you're an Orvis aficionado, ask them for the one that most closely resembles it.

The Cortland Pro-line rods of eight and eight-and-a-half feet are dandies and so are the new offerings from L.L. Bean. Loomis rods can be had in nearly every configuration imaginable, and a letter describing exactly what you desire will most likely be answered affirmatively.

I must make special note of the multi-piece rods as made by

the Deerfield Rod Company of, yes, Deerfield, Massachusetts. Dave Sylvester, the company's owner and chief rod builder, set out some ten years ago to make a series of four-piece rods that could be carried easily under the arm. The idea of a four-piece rod is not a new one, but until the Deerfields came along there were few multi-section rods worth a hoot. They were all too wishy-washy or favored the other extreme. Using Fisher blanks, Dave fussed with the tapers until he got what he liked. His current top-of-the-line rods are the twin-tip models. These rods, in various lengths from seven to nine feet, are four pieces which come with two extra tip sections. By switching the top two pieces, one can accommodate four or five different line weights. Deerfield sells an eight-and-a-half-footer, for example, that will cast five-, six-, seven-, and eight-weight lines by switching tips.

And what of bamboo rods today? Some are being made, of course, probably more per year than was the case in 1972. Most of them are solid, functional fishing tools, and with the new glues they are more durable than cane rods of a half century ago. Perhaps it's simply my tendency to curmudgeonness that brings me to think today's cane rods don't fish as well as they used to. Maybe it's because graphite rods fish so well that I'm looking for something that never was. A few custom rod makers here and there are fashioning fine quality bamboo rods, and of course, Orvis is still in the thick of things. I don't have access to the numbers, but I'd guess that Orvis sells as many cane rods as any maker in the world. Orvis rods remain good values. Their action is *different*. Orvis bamboo rods usually bend in a full curve that allows easy casting for short distances — ideal for most trout streams and small rivers. Being quite soft, they hook fish well, too. For night fishing, however, I've never used an Orvis cane rod that was well suited to my usual two- and three-fly arrangement. Some of the older "light salmon rods" might be perfect, but I've never used one. But mind you, rod action is totally subjective.

The best bamboo rods I've seen produced during the past ten years have come from Thomas and Thomas. Not only do they fish well, but the reel seats, the windings, the varnish finish and other details combine to form the finest cane rods made in the world today. Some of their light trout rods, like the old Leonards, are a bit wispy of tip to hold up to the rigors of night fishing, but two of their models are right on target. One is the "Classic," an eight-and-one-half-footer for the seven-weight line, and the other is the "Individualist," a light salmon rod for the seven- or eight-weight line. These rods cost, respectively, about $800 and $1000 — give or take some small change. Not cheap, of course, but amortized over a few seasons of fishing, who's going to care? Thomas and Thomas also make high quality graphite rods, and their "Big Horn" nine-footer is a dandy.

The more I think about rods, the less sure I become as to how to describe the perfect night fly rod. I've used the word *sensitive* several times by now, and I'm not sure that it conveys all that I mean. Perhaps it doesn't, but when you've had opportunities to fish with a number of different rods, you come to know instantly when one rod has it and another doesn't. If you know what I'm talking about, then fine, you know what I'm talking about.

I'll leave the subject of rods with one final thought. Be sure to get a rod that has a keeper ring just ahead of the grip. Sticking the big flies into the grip will soon rip the cork to shreds. Rig your leader to such a length that it extends exactly from tip-top to keeper ring. Then you will always know that with one pull on your reel you'll be ready to start false casting. Doing this will also prevent the heavy butt section of the leader from developing a permanent kink where it bends around the tip-top guide.

The line used for night work should usually be a floater. The end of the line will probably sink a bit from the weight of the larger wet flies, and this is especially true if you use two or three flies. There may be some special situations in which a commercial sink-tip line will be an advantage. One such situation might be when you want to switch to small flies and get them down deep in a hurry. A one-hundred-percent sinking line is tough enough to lift out of the water at any time. Load it with a couple of number-6 flies and you'll have nothing but casting difficulties.

When white lines came out some years ago, fly fishermen cast a cold traditional eye on them and predicted that they'd never catch on. Scare the fish and all that. Time has proved that they were wrong, and any fly fisherman who doesn't have a white line today isn't with it. It is an especially good choice for the nighttime angler. The pure-white color will catch and reflect any available light and make the line far more visible. Although much of the skill required for night fishing depends on your sense of touch, a visible line can certainly help. This is especially true when you're playing the fish and have him close to your boot tops. Some of the fluorescent orange lines are also excellent in this respect. They are highly visible, and I am sure they don't bother the fish one bit.

Vinyl coated fly lines have been improved considerably over the past few years, and with decent care they will last about three seasons of normal use. I can't really come up with many new ideas concerning lines, except to tout the Cortland 444-XL. All of the major line makers turn out outstanding products, but I've become quite fond of these bright lime-green lines. The finish on these is a bit "harder" than that of other lines, and they won't kink or wind if some slack gathers around your feet. The 444-XL doesn't have that soft "buttery" feel that the regular 444 or the Scientific Angler lines seem to have. Fishermen who use small wet flies and who do a lot of manipulating with the hand-twist retrieve won't care much for the 444-XL, but the night fisherman, the salmon angler, the bass bugger, and the saltwater fly rodder will discover that 10 to 15 more feet of line can be cast with ease. Now, this isn't all that important for the night angler, but the harder finish will help get that line back on the reel when fighting a big trout, and the fluorescent-green color is easier to see than a white line. That can be very important.

One tip worth remembering is that a hardware store product, *Armorall*, is the best thing I've found for "slicking" a tired line. It cleans the line and protects it from insect repellent (a fly line's worst enemy) and any other gunk that may be encountered. For lines only, a can of Armorall will last about a century.

The style of line best suited for night fishing is undoubtedly the double taper. It has the same advantages for the night fly fisherman as it has for the daytime angler. That is, it can be swapped end for end, so that in effect you have two lines for the price of one, and it's much easier to handle than a weight forward line on the average-length casts that are the rule in night fishing.

There isn't much new information that I can offer concerning reels. Most reels used to good advantage by day will work for the night angler. The most important thing to consider is the fit of the reel spool to the frame. There should be no gap there. The slightest opening will allow the line to find its way into the hole, and then you're in big trouble, particularly if a big trout happens to choose that moment to snatch your fly. I have a 1494 Pflueger Medalist that has been in almost constant use for twenty years. I have re-enameled it several times, but nothing more. The click adjustment has always worked perfectly. So have all the other moving parts. I guess it's clear that I like Medalist reels. Your choice of a reel is not really too important so long as you choose one that's well constructed and, for my taste, has a noisy click. A perfectly silent reel is an abomination that should not be tolerated by any fly fisherman. If it were not for the resounding click and the screeching whine that a fish produces when making that first run, outdoor writers would be a terribly frustrated lot. Have you ever heard a fly-rodding story that didn't have at least one reference to a "screaming reel"?

The leader requirements for the night fisherman are also elementary. You simply start with a piece of monofilament closely approximating your line in diameter, and taper down in two-foot sections until you get to a six-or eight-pound tippet. If you use a big dry fly after dark, you may want to go a bit finer but only because the heavier diameters will not go through the hook eye.

Checking some of the old monofilament leader material I used to use, I discovered that it was rope-like when compared with today's chemical strands. Six-pound test (most of it) in the 50's, for example, was nearly as thick as today's 12-pound test. That "mikes" out to nearly .012 inches. The pound test of the night leader, though, is not nearly so important as its diameter. Theoretically, one can go down to six-pound material and have a tippet of .009. But practically, going so fine as that for night fishing (and larger) flies is not good practice. In the first place, flies of size 6 and larger don't cast well on leaders much lighter than .010 and wrap around the body of the leader in a most complex way. Enough things can happen after dark without having to worry about leader tangles.

A basic night leader consists of the following: Twenty inches of .020, 20 inches of .017, 12 inches of .015, 12 inches of .013 and 20 inches of .012. If you want to switch to dry flies, shorten the .012 section a bit and tie on a 24-inch piece of .010.

Manufacturer specifications are different for different pound tests, but, thank goodness, most of them print the diameter on the leader package — and that's the key. To repeat: don't worry about pound test . . . the night angler must always assume he's after big game.

When you construct your night fly leader, allow a trailing end of the barrel knot to extend for approximately eight inches at one or two of the jointures. Here's where the second fly or second and third flies will be attached. Of course, if you change dropper flies frequently, you'll soon discover that you have a very short stub on which to attach the fly. A new section must be tied in. Some fishermen get around this inconvenience by carrying several prepared leaders with flies already attached. This is a good system if you have the patience and memory to always keep the spare casts on hand. I'm usually far too impatient to go fishing, so I very seldom get around to it. Not too many years ago, all wet-fly fishing was done with snelled flies. There was some excuse for snells back when hook manufacturers did not know how to produce eyed hooks. For the fisherman with very poor eyesight, there may be an excuse today, but that would be the only exception.

Probably the most controversial item that a night fisherman carries is his flashlight. In truth, the night fisherman should not carry a flashlight at all. I say this because it is extremely difficult for him to overcome a desire to use it for each and every little reason that pops into his head. Nothing will put down fish more quickly at night than some idiot practicing Morse code. If you can limit yourself to using a flashlight only when changing flies and for finding your way back to the car, carry one, but make it a two-cell job and be sure that the batteries are half worn out when you put them in. An old gentleman with whom I fished a great deal once described the perfect night fisherman's flashlight as one that would surely burn out before he got back to the car.

The night fisherman carries no net. Those foolish little butterfly-catching devices that most eastern anglers are prone to drape around their necks are only suitable for trout of ten inches or smaller. The night fly fisherman must expect bigger game.

Oh, yes, there is also one other small item that will prove valuable for the after-dark angler, and that is a sheepskin or felt-lined fly book. I prefer the book to the metal box because if you drop a fly book, it will float. Those delightful little metal boxes with the fancy little spring clips are just dandy for displaying salmon flies, or, for that matter, night flies — but they will sink like a rock.

THE NIGHT FLY

I am convinced that night fishing for trout was brought to its highest degree of perfection in the headwater region of the Allegheny River. Potter County was the mother lode of this specialized sport. Where else in the world is any wet fly larger than a size 10 always referred to as "a night fly"? In fact, during my youth it was common to identify all small flies as "day" flies, and this was not a corruption of "may" fly but rather a local expression that indicated that this was indeed night-fly country.

The man who probably did most for the sport of fishing after dark with flies was Doctor Samuel A. Phillips, of Coudersport, Pennsylvania. He was a dentist but seldom practiced in the mouths of human beings. He was far more interested in attaching bits of steel to the jaws of trout. His wife was a fly tier, and she supplied all of Doc's flies. Because he practiced dentistry so seldom, her fly sales to other fishermen made up the largest part of their income. An ideal arrangement, I always thought, and a great contribution to angling history.

Caroline Larrabee Phillips' flies were beautifully made, but unfortunately most of them were tied with gut snells on eyeless hooks, and few of them have survived. The small handful that I have managed to acquire are perfect examples of the art. The style is most graceful, and the hooks (maker unknown) are excellent. It should be noted that the general quality of fly hooks was as good — perhaps better — sixty years ago as it is today. She tied many standard patterns of that era and many that are still popular, but the most interesting of all were those that were developed by her husband for the special purpose of night fishing.

The Yellow Dun was the most famous of Mrs. Phillips' flies. This pattern probably started out as a brook-trout fly, since that was the native trout of the land, but somewhere along the line when brown trout began to flourish in Pennsylvania waters it was discovered that here indeed was the king of the night flies. After the Phillips family moved to California in 1920, the supply of these flies was used up and only a few were saved. I have one of the original Yellow Duns. I wouldn't take a fortune for it, at least not until I finally figure out what the ingredients really are. The wing is nothing more than a gray duck secondary. The hackle is medium ginger. It's the body material that is the secret ingredient. When dry, it is a rosy-pink mohair sort of thing, but when wet it takes on the appearance of a glob of bloody flesh. After his supply of Yellow Duns disappeared, Bob Pinney tried desperately to get fly manufacturers and dealers in fly-tying materials to come up with a good substitute. He never succeeded, and perhaps the secret of the body material died with Mrs. Phillips in California.

This whole account would be but another interesting fish story were it not for the documented evidence of the amazing catches made on the Yellow Dun. Since there isn't anything yellow about the fly, nor is it dun colored, its name is also a mystery. It outfished every other fly of the period by a wide margin, and facsimiles of the pattern are still good today. About forty years ago the Phillips Company (no relationship with Doc Phillips) of Alexandria, Pennsylvania, supplied a version of this pattern to Ridlon's hardware store in Coudersport, Pennsylvania, which they marketed under the name of Ridlon's Special. This pattern had wings of lemon wood duck with pink angora fur for the body. It worked quite well but not nearly as well as the original, or so I've been told by old-timers who have used both. I've never had the pleasure of fishing with one of the original Yellow Duns, but I have used the Ridlon's Special and some other substitutes that I have concocted, and they certainly are effective.

Another one of Mrs. Phillips' popular patterns, though it probably was not her invention, was the New Page. This fly featured a brilliant tangerine wing with a body of buckskin wound with the smooth side out and ribbed with fine gold wire. An outlandish-looking creation, to be sure, but it's another very effective night fly pattern that originally started out as a brook-trout fly. Some fly fishermen hold the reasonable assumption that the New Page was merely another attempt to imitate a brook-trout fin.

The stories have it that Doc Phillips fished for big browns at night in a fashion similar to that used for brook trout during the early 1900s: with a quartering cast downstream and a jerk-and-stop retrieve. He caught a lot of trout but never did he get any of the real monsters that were caught by Pinney and others after night fishing was developed into a more sophisticated game. Pinney always believed that the reason Doc never caught a brown trout of over eighteen inches was that he used flies that were too small. Doc invariably fished three flies, usually size 10s, occasionally size 12s, and very rarely size 8s. When I first began after-dark angling in 1944, size 6 was the standard, with 4s and 2s being used fairly often. In most freestone water, number 6s would be the choice today.

Before we get into a further discussion of night-fly patterns, I'd like to touch on the matter of what trout seem to think these large flies are. As I mentioned earlier, some mayflies hatch after dark, as do many other aquatic and terrestrial insects. Add to this the brown trout's appetite for nymphs, crayfish, and minnows, and for that matter, for practically any creature small enough for him to swallow, and it becomes clear that his nighttime diet is quite varied. But simple hunger does not explain it all. As we'll see in a moment, some of the most effective night-fly patterns could not possibly be considered imitations of something good to eat. There must be other reasons.

Frequently (in fact, during certain periods, invariably), large night-caught trout will have empty stomachs, indicating that they had not been feeding when the night fly that captured them drifted by. And when, during the same evening, as I have done, you catch three trout, none of which have anything in its stomach, you begin to find their reasons for striking very puzzling. Fear, curiosity, or just downright aggressiveness may be the answer.

There's something akin to Atlantic salmon fishing in the night-fishing game. These ocean-running cousins of the brown trout don't feed while they are in fresh water, yet they will take a brightly colored fly when the presentation suits them. Exactly the same situation occurs at night with many big browns and, to a lesser degree, with brooks and rainbows when they occur in waters where they are outnumbered by browns.

Fly presentation to trout at night is frequently just as critical as it is to Atlantic salmon at all times. Leader diameter can make a difference, but it usually does not. The angle at which the trout first sees the fly and the movements of the fly after that are far more important than the size of the tippet. That is, an angler who uses a twelve-pound-test leader but who casts his flies in the right place at the right time will do better than an angler who shows the trout a delicate leader but casts his flies in the wrong place at the wrong time. Now let's move on to some more talk about favorite flies.

Topping the list of all-time night fly favorites is a trio that should be dealt with together: the Silver Doctor, the Governor, and the Professor. These three flies are quite different, yet all three will sometimes take trout on the same night. On other occasions, the trout will show a decided preference for one or the other. These three flies in sizes 4, 6, and 8 are essentials for night fly fishermen. The Professor and the Governor are pretty much standardized, being tied in nearly the same way by everyone. (The only variation might be in the thickness of the peacock-herl body on the Governor. The herl should always be tied on amply to provide a fat, buggy appearance.) The Silver Doctor is another matter. There are scores of variations on this old standard salmon fly. I examined one Scottish version of the Silver Doctor that had a least twenty-five different materials used in its construction.

Such exuberance is not necessary for the construction of a very workable night "S.D." The version I have settled on contains a tail of golden pheasant crest, a red wool tag, an embossed-tinsel body, wood duck wings, and mixed blue and guinea hackles. Of course, like most tiers, I juggled the components around from time to time, but that is pretty much my standard pattern. Although any of these flies may work at any time during the night-fly season, they could be grouped by effectiveness during the season: Governor — early season; Professor — mid-season; Silver Doctor — late season.

For early season night fishing — that is, from approximately May 15th to June 25th — the darker night-fly patterns will generally be most effective. The proven favorites are these: Fiery Brown, Black Dose, Lord Baltimore, Hardy's Favorite, Black Prince, Lead Wing Coachman, Red Rogue, and Montreal. As the season progresses and we reach the middle of the night-fly season — the end of June through July — the best patterns are a bit more brilliant, with the barred mallard wing playing a decided part in the fly's effectiveness. In this group we find the Grizzly King, Rube Wood, King of the Waters, Queen of the Waters, Royal Coachman (duck quill or hair wing), Cosseboom, and Blue Charm. When we come to the tail end of the season — August and later — the previously mentioned Silver Doctor becomes the number-one choice. The rest of the flies that produce during this last period are no less brilliant. They include the Silver Blue, Tomah Joe, Thunder and Lighting, Jock Scott, Gray Hackle Silver, and Black Gnat Silver.

I am sure that to the average fly fisherman these patterns will seem a rather bizarre assortment, and especially so when brown trout are considered. If cast toward a large brown in the daytime, such patterns would very likely put him down for the rest of the day. A few, notably the Coachman and the Gray Hackle, have gained some reputation as good daytime flies when used in smaller sizes. Some of the other flies would probably be good daytime trout patterns too, but they certainly were not developed for that purpose.

The student of fly patterns will immediately notice that some time-tested Atlantic-salmon patterns are included in this night-fly list. There are times when these gaudily dressed hooks will outfish the more somber dressings. In fact, that's how the Silver Doctor gained notoriety as a night trout fly. The original Silver Doctors used in the East for night fishing came to the United States from Britain, by way of the salmon rivers of Canada. Local versions of these salmon patterns have evolved, but it was the original ties that earned them their reputations.

Commercially tied salmon flies can be a problem, however. The standard-weight salmon hooks are a bit too heavy for most trout work. They sink rapidly and become easily hung up on the bottom. If you dress your own flies, you can eliminate this problem by using standard-weight wet-fly hooks or light-wire low-water salmon hooks. Or you can run a loop of monofilament from beneath the eye to the hook point, turn it around the point, and tie it in at the tail section. This serves as a weed and rock guard of sorts and allows you to fish your flies right on the bottom, when that method seems to be producing. This strand of mono does not seem to interfere with the strike.

The student of fly-patterns will note that in nearly all of my suggested night flies (there are many more good ones), one or more of three materials will be found. These are peacock herl, gold or silver tinsel, and a bit of red. The red may take the form of feather, wool, or floss. In fact, most of the truly outstanding night fly patterns have two of these materials included in their make-up. The effectiveness of red is easily explained by the trout's predatory instinct. All creatures that prey upon other creatures are attracted by the color of blood. The amount of red used appears to be critical. But an all-red fly usually produces about as well as an all-yellow or an all-blue fly, which is to say not very well at all. The hint of red on the Governor or the red spray of feather in the wing of the Jock Scott seem to be more to the trout's liking. The usefulness of tinsel might be explained by its suggestion of the flash of a small bait fish. I have long preferred silver tinsel to gold. I haven't experimented with mylar a great deal, but the use of mylar piping material appears to have a great future in the creation of night flies. Peacock herl has historically been a favored body material for trout flies. It possesses an iridescent quality and a buggy appearance that trout find very fetching. In selecting flies, or herl if you happen to be a fly tier, always look for a peacock feather that favors the green. It is usually much fluffier and has a far more lifelike quality than the feathers referred to as "bronze." Like all fly-tying feathers these days, good quality peacock herl is becoming difficult to obtain.

Generally, the materials used for night flies should be soft in texture but positive of color. The reds should be real reds and the Silver Doctor blue should be a very vibrant shade, but no material should be of dry-fly stiffness. Soft materials should be used because a trout may occasionally pick up the fly on a slack line and hold it for an instant before the angler realizes the fish is there. This is still another similarity to Atlantic-salmon fishing. If the hackle, wing, and tail are extremely stiff, the night-taken fly may be ejected before the angler has a chance to strike. However, the very soft strike is not the rule at night. We'll discuss various types of strike a bit later.

Another broad rule of thumb is that flies dressed especially for night fishing should be tied quite full. An extra portion of soft hackle, a chunkier body, and a more generous wing will usually gather more strikes than a sparsely dressed fly. There are occasions very late in the season, or during extremely low water, when a sparsely tied fly would prove best, but trout, particularly large ones, are looking for a substantial meal at night, and the "low-water ties" usually come out second best. With all of these patterns, and no matter where you fish, your initial selection should be predominantly of size 6s. A six-inch brook trout or a ten-pound brown can seize this size quite readily. If you become really serious about night fishing, some 4s and 2s should be added, especially in the favored three patterns, as well as a scattering of 8s and 10s. In the smaller flies, the fancier patterns, particularly those with tinsel, will be the most effective.

While I cannot bring myself to deny the universal value of size-6 wet flies for night fishing, some recent experiences (over the past 15 years) have proven the need to carry some larger flies. Because my mentors fished mostly with sixes, I did, too, and seldom found other sizes necessary. But thinking back, perhaps we should have tried more monster-size bunches of fur and feathers. Bringing trout up from deeper pools and giving them fits of excitement in shallow stretches can sometimes be done with huge flies when the smaller ones won't get a look. I must admit I honestly didn't buy this advice a dozen years ago — except on rare occasions when absolutely nothing buggy was on the scene.

One sultry July evening found me on the Yellow Breeches, just downstream from the bridge at Bowmansdale, Pennsylvania. The stream there was heavily stocked in April, but by this time most of the stocked fish were gone and so were the fishermen. But a few big resident browns were always there and so were a reasonable supply of smallmouth bass. As full darkness set in, some mighty splashes and swirls indicated bass. I had no idea what they were rising for since I couldn't see a single bug of any kind on the surface or in the air. But some *big* fish were working, and that was enough for me. I tried the usual string of three night flies and was rewarded with nothing. A size-8 Royal Wulff drummed up one ten-inch bass, and I would have given up the evening, except for the fact that even more fish were wildly splashing about. I had just returned from an Atlantic salmon trip and had a huge Bomber stuck in the sheepskin pad on my vest. I mean it was big. About three-and-a-half inches long and fat as a Polish sausage. What the hell . . . give it a shot.

On about the third cast, the rod was nearly jerked out of my hand, and a three-pound smallmouth jumped three times before I could raise the tip. Two more bass quickly followed, and the fourth strike created a cave in the surface that looked like someone had thrown a Shetland Pony into the pool. No jumps from this one, though, and the fish promptly headed downstream with a heavy surge.

For a trout in a small stream, it was one of the few I've hooked that got into my backing. I knew it was a trout because it nearly beached itself getting to the next downstream pool. The form of the trout was clearly visible as it flopped and flipped through a short piece of shallow water, and I gulped several times at its length. With the 10-pound leader and big hook (that Bomber was tied on a size-2 long shank), I really "put the wood to him" and within a few minutes skidded the racy brown onto a sandbar. The trout was a hook-beaked male that measured a full 28 inches. It wasn't a fat fish — it only weighted six-and-a-half pounds — but the head was alligatorish and its mouth could have held two softballs. That big bomber was nearly lost in the cavernous maw and was deep in the throat. That fish wanted the big fly badly!

The salmon Bombers, big Muddlers, huge deer hair bass bugs, and frogs have all taken big trout at night, and more would be taken on them if anglers would remember that night-feeding fish are always on the lookout for a substantial meal. There's no need to worry about small fish when casting such giant flies. The little guys can't wrap their mouths around them. The regular night-fly patterns that I previously mentioned are also effective in jumbo sizes, particularly those with peacock-herl bodies. In order to achieve extra body thickness in these flies, wind black or green wool around the hook shanks until you come close to the diameter wanted. Then, wind four or five strands of thick herl on top of each fly, apply some head cement to the wool, and bind the herl down with tying silk for additional durability. These flies won't be collectors' items, but they will hang together.

Streamers

When I tried not to be dogmatic about flies and fly types in the first go around of this book, rereading has revealed that I wasn't. I have been taken to task by fellow anglers, angling friends with whom I have not fished, and other citizen anglers for my negative pronouncements concerning streamer flies at night. Here again, my heros, whom I slavishly chose to emulate, didn't use them after dark, so I didn't either. I was wrong.

Streamers will indeed catch fish at night. There is, however, some "how-to", I find, which must be inserted. How one fishes a streamer at night is most important. Assuming that larger fish are what we're after, those streamers must be fished far more deliberately than one would work a long fly during the daytime hours. Since streamers are created with a minnow-shape in mind, it must be understood that a darting minnow, moving here and there in a nervous fashion, is not the sort of prey a wise old brown spends much time pursuing. Streamers fished at night must move with a slow, measured cadence that suggests an easy meal. Stripping a streamer through the water in rapid jerk-jerk-jerk twitches will catch a smallish trout, perhaps a lot of them, but the wall-hangers won't pay much attention.

The patterns that work best are those that are long enough to suggest a minnow but bulky enough to be mistaken for a crayfish. Sculpin patterns are perfect if tied with a full head and a tad of olive-brown fur. Size 2 is perfect. Green Muddlers, Black Wooly Buggers and various maribous with brown or black bodies are also good producers.

The trick in fishing these big streamers is to allow the fly to sink to the bottom and then creep it along in extremely slow, one-inch jumps. No kidding — *one-inch strips*. Any faster than this and the fish simply won't respond. Weighted flies don't work well because the fly is hung up ninety percent of the time. And besides, a weighted fly doesn't have the lifelike quality a good streamer should have. (Let me hasten to insert that I do use weighted flies from time to time in heavy water when they must be used, but I'd rather not if I can avoid it.)

Those who have fished in New Zealand, Australia and Tasmania tell me wonderful tales of night fishing with the famous Matuka streamers and large fly patterns such as Mrs. Parson and Red Setter. I have not fished "down under," but it comes as no surprise that the browns there are nocturnal feeders. Actually, from the cold of Patagonia to the sea trout rivers of the Arctic and in between, brown trout of substantial size lean towards a more proper dinner hour.

In any impoundment where available food and water temperature bring trout, bass, or walleyes into water less than 12 feet deep, night fishing with streamer flies can be highly effective. Fish in lakes, and particularly the various salmons, are fond of minnows, mostly because they're frequently the most available form of substantial food. Casting from shore or from a boat toward the shore can be productive once the right depth is discovered.

I once had a great night of fishing for pound-and-a-half brookies in O'Neill Flow Pond in New York State by casting a size-6 Black Ghost from the shore. A forty-foot cast would drop the streamer into about eight feet of water. With a sink-tip line, a count of one to twelve (about a second per number) allowed the fly to touch bottom. Then, in slow, short jerks, with the rod tip held low, the fly would be retrieved spasmodically into the shallows. The brookies would usually hit just as the fly was about to touch the shoreline, causing me to believe that they were following it for at least 25 feet before striking. Exciting fishing!

This same technique with this same fly is very productive on a number of lakes and ponds. Walleyes and bass like the Black Ghost, too, and if I had to choose one streamer fly for the rest of my days, it would surely be the Black Ghost. I'm not sure if the fish always think the Black Ghost is a minnow, because there are a lot of other aquatic and land creatures which are black. But the natural white hackles laid over the black body ribbed with tinsel does indeed present a slick-looking minnow silhouette. I tie most of my Black Ghosts with five saddle hackles attached in such a way to have the ends of the wing feathers barely reaching the bend of the 3X long hook. In Maine and other parts of the U.S. and Canada, it's the fashion to tie streamers a bit longer, with the hackle wing feathers extending well beyond the hook. Fish will go for these longer flies, but in my experience it's much more difficult to hook them. This can be rectified somewhat by using a "stinger" hook attached with a short piece of monofilament, trailing it behind and just beneath the tip of the wing. This idea works well for trolled flies, but if much casting is done, the wing feathers tend to twist around the stinger hook and foul up the presentation — and the leader as well.

Streamer flies are handsome to the eye when tied with thin, beautifully tapered bodies and delicate, wispy wings. For night fishing, however, the fat, chunky body will do much better. For my Black Ghosts, I use black wool or fur for the bodies instead of floss, for more bulk, and, since I love the material, I also tie a variation of the Black Ghost with peacock herl. While some highly skilled anglers will disagree, I strongly believe that painted eyes on streamers or the addition of a jungle cock eye or snippet of black and white wood duck will bring more strikes.

Dry Flies

Dry flies after dark present a most confounding problem right off the bat. How in the world are you going to see a floating fly when you have difficulty seeing your rod tip? Surprisingly enough, a size-12 dry fly can be spotted on moderately smooth water even on a moonless night. If the angler is along the stream during the transition from daylight to darkness, his night vision can become quite sharp indeed. If you avoid flashing a match, cigarette lighter, or flashlight in front of your eyes, you will discover that you can see quite well, particularly if you are familiar with the area in the daytime. There are times, especially during a nocturnal hatch of mayflies, when the dry fly can be very productive. Drag is not nearly so important a factor at night. The large, fluffy dry fly can be manipulated after dark in a fashion that would be completely unproductive during the daytime. However, large wets will usually do just as well as the floaters for surface-feeding night trout, and the overall percentage of hooked fish will be much greater with the sunken fly. Trout taking the dry fly at night seem to have a pretty poor batting average. Frequently there will be a huge splash followed by the angler's strike, but no fish will be hooked. The trout's marksmanship in taking something off the surface appears to suffer at night. Perhaps it is an optical problem, and then again it may be just a last-minute rejection.

I don't mean to completely run down the use of dry flies at night. There are times when nothing else will work quite as well. During a Green Drake hatch that lasts on into the night, a size-8 or size-10 dry Light Cahill can do a land-office business. There are some other dry patterns that are fine for night work, notably the Wulff series and the Badger and White Spiders, but by far the most effective dry I have ever used at night has been the Light Cahill. Because you're sure to strike harder at night, use a tippet no lighter than 2X. A seven-and-a-half-foot leader is adequate.

Special-Purpose Flies

There are some special-purpose flies that really can't be considered either dry or wet but which also have a place in the night fisherman's kit. Foremost of these is the Muddler Minnow. The Muddler is a most effective night fly, especially if there are grasshoppers about. Grasshoppers probably don't often find their way into the water after dark, but the trout certainly remember what they look like. The Muddler does a fine job of suggesting this large insect. My favorite method of fishing the Muddler is to dress the whole fly with dry-fly floatant and retrieve it slowly, twitching it to make it duck under and bob to the surface. A pattern that is tied in pretty much the same way is the Black Cricket. This creation, formulated in the Letort region of Pennsylvania, is nothing more than a Black Muddler tied a bit short. Another fly in this fuzzy-headed category is the sculpin imitation created by Dave Whitlock of Bartlesville, Oklahoma. This fly had it beginnings on the pages of *Field & Stream* magazine as part of an original streamer-fly collection. Various fly tiers throughout the United States were asked to dream up totally new conceptions to imitate North American bait fish. One of the minnows Whitlock drew was the sculpin. The pattern he came up with is one of the most effective flies I have ever seen or fished. It certainly looks like a sculpin when it's wet, and when fished on top or in the surface it resembles any number of wiggling creatures that might find their way into the water.

I remarked earlier in the book that the so-called whumpus

fly is the thing that many fly fishermen remember. Trout, and big ones too, have been caught after dark on every conceivable pattern, from the Abbey to the Zulu. As you progress as a night fisherman, certain flies will come to be your favorite. You may even come up with another Yellow Dun.

GEORGE HARVEY'S "PUSHER" FLIES

While some of our angling "heros" go out of their way to deny it, there is considerable dogma scattered throughout their pronouncements. On such and such a day a certain fly must be fished in a certain way with a certain leader and with specified tackle. There's nothing really wrong with all of this waltzing about; it makes good reading, and when properly applied, almost any piece of angling advice can be useful. George Harvey does have some rather positive ideas about how to fish for trout under a variety of conditions, but I have yet to meet another fisherman of equal experience and skill who is less set in his ways. At 75, Harvey is still learning and teaching and one of the most enthusiastic anglers one could hope to meet.

For nearly 40 years, George Harvey was the fly fishing instructor at Penn State University. During that period he shepherded 35,000 students through the mysteries of fly tying and fly fishing via his special course, which was a bona fide part of the curriculum at Penn State. To earn his keep, he also coached track and soccer teams there and eventually became head of student physical education. But it was the fishing course that held the greater part of his attention. What a job!

Teaching fly fishing allowed Harvey to spend working time at what he did during most of his free time. With a lifetime packed full of more fishing hours than most of us can only dream about, one would have to learn a thing or two about fly fishing. Harvey not only learned, he learned with gusto, and blessed with a brain that catalogs events and places like a computer, he's retained a vast store of techniques and tips that guarantee his position among American angling greats.

George Harvey graduated from Penn State in 1935 with a degree in Ornamental Horticulture. "There probably wasn't a worse degree to have in those days," he chuckles at the recollection. "The country was in the middle of economic chaos, and growing nice bushes and flowers was not something most folks were thinking about. I was not greeted with many job offers."

While attending college, Harvey took a job at one of the college fraternity houses. He came to know the dean of the school of forestry, who was also an ardent fisherman. On the opening day of the 1933 trout season, the dean invited young George to accompany him to Spring Creek. As it turned out, the dean caught a couple of stocked brook trout, and George took a basketful of sizable browns. The dean's were caught on worms while George did his fishing with wet flies. Impressed by this performance, the dean invited George to establish a course in fly tying and fly fishing. After graduating, he did. Harvey retired in 1972 from this labor of love, but the course survives under the able directorship of a Harvey protege, Joe Humphreys.

In the mountainous regions of Pennsylvania, trout fishing was nearly a form of religion. Any boy growing up in such environs couldn't avoid exposure, and for many of them, the sport was happily embraced. It also followed that role models were frequently those "fishing heros" who lived close by, and a few who didn't. Aspiring anglers were blessed by geography in a state that held Charlie Fox, Vince Marinaro, John Alden Knight, Jim Liesinring, and a respectable cadre of lesser-known, but equally proficient, flycasters. George Harvey knew this and set out to probe as many Pennsylvania streams as possible. He expanded his fishing excursions to many other ports of call over the years, but his intimate knowledge of Keystone State waters has grown to encyclopedic proportions.

I first met George Harvey about 25 years ago. I had known of his fame at Penn State and that he was a fly fisherman of some regard, but we did not have the chance to talk at length until three years ago. As we rambled on about fish and fishing it suddenly dawned on me that Harvey was doing a lot of recalling about the streams in the northcentral part of Pennsylvania. These were *my* streams, the streams I grew up on and on which I first discovered the thrills of latching onto brown trout of heroic size while night fishing. I had fished these places during the 50s and 60s. He had fished the very same pools during the 30s and 40s. A twenty-year age difference in chronological and angling years. I'll admit that I tested George's veracity a time or two as we talked about the Goodsell Hole, Seven Bridges, the long pool below the Chestnut Street bridge, and the famous Balknap Pool on the upper Allegheny. I nearly fell out of my chair as he not only nodded familiarity at the mention of these names but proceeded to describe subtle landmarks, reference points, and specific stumps and snags and how the currents moved in various parts of individual pools! He had been at these places long before I had and knew them intimately. I was embarrassed to have played amateur detective and interrogator.

In the matter of dry-fly fishing, George Harvey is a firm believer in a "soft" presentation. He is much more interested in size than color, but he's quick to point out that the right color combined with the right size will always give the angler an advantage. "A 30-foot cast is about all the trout fisherman needs on 90 percent of the trout water in the world . . . if the fly lands softly and doesn't drag. I've never believed that ultrafine leaders helped very much. I use mostly 4X and 5X tippets and seldom use a leader much longer than nine or nine-and-a-half feet. The trout see your leader no matter what diameter it is, and as long as the tippet will bend and flex with the current in order to prevent drag, most trout won't be spooked by it."

A heap of anglers, and good ones, too, won't buy all of this as a package. Harvey agrees that longer casts are needed on some western and not a few eastern streams, but he still stresses getting as close to the fish as possible and dropping the fly softly. "I use a much lighter leader butt than most fly fishermen and build my leaders with 20-inch sections tapering down to .009 or .007. I make most casts in the pull-back or check manner — that is, lift the rod tip just before the fly reaches the water in a way that makes the fly fall gently instead of hitting hard."

As good as Harvey is with the dry fly, and he is very good, his fame as a nighttime angler was legendary four decades ago. My infatuation with stalking big browns at night during my teenage and young adult years was almost in the danger zone. I couldn't get enough of it. George was captured by it, too, but curiously, his experiences on the very same streams I fished led him down a slightly different trail.

My early fishing mentors fished with size-6 wet flies, usually two or three of them on a cast, while George favored larger flies fished singly. Oh, he also fished standard wets at night, but over the years he came to think that at night larger trout struck more frequently on huge flies than they did on small sunken flies. That's an arguable point, as is any aspect of fly fishing, but Harvey's success on his not-so-well-known "pusher flies" is considerable.

In 1973, when *Night Fishing For Trout* was first printed, perhaps less than 3000 copies of the book were manufactured. Interested in such things, George Harvey bought a copy, just to compare notes, of course, and soon after sent me a couple samples of the strangest-looking flies I'd seen up to that time. With the package of flies was a note.

"I discovered while reading your new book that you don't think too highly of dry flies for use at night. For many years I wasn't too keen on them either, so I set about designing some that I thought would do better. They have. Here are a few for you to try. Good fishing after dark."

The flies arrived about the middle of August, when I had been enjoying some excellent night fishing on the Yellow Breeches. I didn't know George Harvey well at that time, but his reputation as an angler was well established. The flies went with me that night, and with a measure of reluctance I tied one on, replacing my usual cast of three size-6 wet flies. On the first cast I snagged an overhanging limb and lost fly number one. Fly number two produced no trout but did seduce a two-pound smallmouth bass. Well now! Harvey's flies are bass catchers to be sure, but brown trout? Probably not. The wet flies were restrung and I went back to business as usual and caught two browns of about 15 inches before closing shop. So much for "pusher flies."

Two years later, I told George of my less-than-stellar performance with his flies and, undaunted, he presented me with a dozen of his best pushers, with the admonition: "Now listen, don't be a stick-in-the-mud. Give these an honest try and see what you think. They'll work, they really will."

The new gift flies were an assortment of colors and sizes, some of them as large as sizes 1 and 2. A bit large, I thought, for eastern trout fishing.

The first chance I had to try them came on a less-than-perfect night. I was on Sinnemahoning Creek. As darkness approached and the sky was about to dump some rain, I rigged a seven-foot leader tapered to six-pound test. Just right, I thought, for one of George's big "hummingbirds." Hummingbirds? They were more the size of sparrows!

My normal string of three wet flies makes a sort of *whoosh-whoosh* sound as they are false cast, but these fluffy monsters sounded more like F-14 fighters buzzing past my ears. But I stuck with them and began to work the tail of the well-proven pool. The rain, more of a steady mist, didn't amount to much. Still, I got soaked, but I didn't mind all that much because within less than an hour I was into a very good fish that had engulfed a size-2 pusher (I didn't tie on the larger one). And what a strike! The way this water caved in around the fly, and the solid run upstream into the deep water, spelled big fish. After a few minutes of deep tugging and another run of thirty feet or so, a bull-headed male brown of about 21 inches lay flopping at my feet. Not bad for my first fish on a George Harvey pusher.

Other experiences with Harvey's big floaters caused me to alter considerably my thinking about dry flies at night. It's not that I didn't use them, but frankly, the fish I'd taken in the past on drys at night had been much smaller than what one expects to catch. On the other hand, perhaps my choices of nighttime floaters had been too small to interest big trout.

George's theory about his pusher flies is that large trout are not terribly interested in small meals. They don't feed all that often, and when they do, as George puts it, "They don't want appetizers, they're looking for the main course."

The bodies of Harvey's pusher flies are of various furs and yarns. All of them are palmer hackled, or fully wound with a hackle feather. The bodies are extremely fat and taper quickly to form a thick silhouette. The tails can be tied in different ways, but he prefers a pair of pheasant breast feathers, the ones with the tiny black triangles at the tip. It's the wings of the pusher that give these flies their generic name. Breast feathers from several different birds can be used as long as they display sufficient "springiness." (The quill has to be tough to hold up to false casting and fish teeth.) Grouse, pheasant, guinea hen, and duck feathers are usually utilized as wings for these big flies.

Care in matching the wings is important to avoid cocking and rolling the fly as it is being pulled through the water. The weight of the fly and placement of the wings at the very front are also factors. As opposed to riding high like a spider or heavily hackled Wulff-type fly, this fly scoots along partially in the water. Flies which coast along on the very tips of their hackles are lovely to watch, but their elevated position makes it much more difficult to hook fish — and this is true, day or night. When a fish rises to seize such a fly, the fish can't help but push a wake of water in front of it's nose, actually pushing the fly out of the trout's "strike zone." This isn't always the case, but it happens often enough to be frustrating. With the pusher flies being half in the water and half out, this cushion of water is much less of a problem and allows the fish to gulp the fly more readily.

While the pusher can't be termed an all-purpose fly, it does have considerable value as a bass fly, day or night, and it has recently been proven as an Atlantic salmon fly. The pusher is not well known in fly-fishing circles. The reason for this is most likely a reluctance on the part of those who have fished with it to let the good news become public knowledge. Because of his generous nature, this hasn't been entirely George Harvey's fault. For many years, he's been telling friends, including me, how to make the fly and recently included instructions for tying it in his handbook, *Trout Fishing and Fly Tying*.

The pusher fly has still another advantage we haven't touched on yet, and here I suspect Harvey of being just a bit devious. We've been talking about this fly being a floater, which it is if dressed well with a good floatant, but the truth is it works just as well — and maybe better — as a wet fly. Fished across and downstream, and not worrying if it floats or sinks, it can perform wonders. As I was writing this I called George to point out that several times while fishing a pusher it sank on me and hooked fish as often as it did while floating. I had assumed that the fly had done its best work as a floater, but with what sounded like a muffled chuckle, George made a confession. "Well, the pusher does take trout on the surface, all right, but actually, I've taken about 90 percent of my night-caught trout on this fly while it was being slowly retrieved *underwater*. The trick is to allow it to reach its maximum swing in the current and then bring it through the water very slowly by stripping in line or with the hand-twitch retrieve. Those pusher wings flex and unflex as the fly is worked, and that action, along with the fat fuzzy body, seems to be very attractive to big trout."

George, you sly fox, you, the pusher is a wet fly after all!

The upshot of this is that the pusher fly can be fished dry, if you prefer, or it can be fished as a traditional wet fly and lobbed with much less false casting which is needed to dry the fly. I'm not accusing George Harvey of withholding information about the pusher being a wet fly as well as a dry . . . I simply didn't ask when I received those first samples. Others who were fishing the pusher fly long before I was didn't volunteer much either. It is reasonably well known, however, that the pushers have accounted for more than a small wagon-load of brown trout well over the two-foot mark. All of them have been taken at night, and I strongly suspect that the fly was underwater when most of the strikes occurred. It is also of no small importance that the largest fly-caught brown trout ever taken in Pennsylvania was caught on a George Harvey pusher. The big fish weighted 15 lbs. 5 oz. and was caught by, of all people, Joe Humphreys, Harvey's replacement and long-time acolyte at Penn State.

Regardless of what is being used at night, the angler must always assume that a fish of more generous proportions is going to strike. Its been proven to me that more strikes will come on size-6 flies than on something larger. It's also been proven that while fewer strikes will be felt on Harvey's pusher flies or on larger wet flies, the fish will be bigger. From a practical standpoint, a ten-inch trout has some problem getting one of these big pushers into his mouth. A small fish may slash at one, but getting hooked probably won't happen.

The American and world fishing stages can count many who have promoted the sport through innovative fishing techniques. I have a feeling that, in time, George Harvey's pusher flies will eventually become as famous as the Wulff series or the Muddler Minnow. It won't happen overnight . . . but it will happen if a few more anglers give these strange-looking flies an honest try. I fooled around for several years before seriously casting them. You shouldn't wait so long.

LIVE BAIT
AND VARIOUS LURES

Certain fly fishermen, and some others who pretend to be strictly flymen, have advised me not to write about the use of natural bait after dark. I must admit that I am tempted to follow their advice, but I would be a long way from the truth if I didn't admit that on some nights natural baits can be almost as good as dynamite. I must also make a confession: I have at times fished with nearly every live, slimy, wiggly creature that exists. (I admit this freely enough, but never without pointing out that the big flies are much more fun to fish than any sort of bait.)

The first bait to consider is the one most easily gathered — the nightcrawler. There are times, particularly after a summer shower, when the nightcrawler is the finest bait available for night trout. A six-inch worm, rigged on a long-shank number-6 hook and allowed to drift freely with the current, can be deadly. Later on in the summer, however, when the water temperature crawls into the lower 70s, the trout seem to lose their taste for them. This is the time when the wise live-bait fisherman turns to crayfish.

These small lobster-like creatures have a soft, buttery consistency and are quite fragile if gathered just after shedding.

The hook should be placed through the tail section as close to the back flippers as possible. Weight the crayfish down with a small splitshot or two, and go to it.

Trout do a lot of minnow chasing after dark, particularly in the slick glides that form at the base of a large pool. After watching a big trout in a surface-zipping pursuit, the fisherman assumes that here would be the ideal place to fish a minnow. In fact, that is the very toughest place in which to make a minnow appear natural to the trout. The head end of a large pool is a much better place for the nighttime minnow fisherman to practice his art. Using one of the small minnow wires with a double number-8 hook, the fisherman can work a dead minnow quite effectively against the current. Old-time minnow fishermen always made sure that the minnow was hooked in such a way that it would rotate on retrieve, as a sort of natural spinning lure.

These three creatures — nightcrawlers, crayfish, and minnows — are the standout nighttime baits. Others that have been used with some success are black salamanders, small lamprey eels, leopard frogs, hellgrammites, and grasshoppers. With any natural bait, the technique can be nothing more than tossing the bait out in a likely looking spot and simply waiting for the fish to find it. But the more effective night bait fishermen impart some sort of movement to their offering. The dead minnow can be jerked through the water quite violently, but the nightcrawler or crayfish should be hand-twist retrieved across the bottom in a lifelike way. When one is fishing very still water, this same sort of retrieve can be used most effectively with a pair of large wet flies. In a situation in which the current doesn't work for you, you must give your fly some lifelike movement to interest the trout.

Trout have been taken after dark on plugs, poppers, and spinners of assorted sizes and shapes. But, oddly enough, any lure, whether it be made of wood, plastic or metal, seems to lose its trout-catching ability in certain waters after one brief flurry of success. The most noteworthy incident of this sort in my experience took place one June night at the famed Good-sell Pool in Potter County, Pennsylvania. Roy Heimel, a local butcher, who fished on occasion, arrived at the pool that night with a $3/8$-ounce frog-colored Flatfish. The regular bait dunkers and night flyers at the pool enjoyed a good round of chuckles when Roy announced that he was going to try the Flatfish that evening. To the amazement of everyone present, he proceeded to catch six brown trout, the smallest being sixteen inches, all taken on the green Flatfish. The next morning, the local hardware stores were inundated with requests for green Flatfish in any size! For two weeks thereafter the trout up and down the Allegheny saw a good deal of this lure, but I haven't heard of one being taken on that particular creation since.

With some variations, this story has been repeated on countless rivers and lakes throughout the world. A new lure, fly, or what-have-you takes the area by storm for a short while, then is abandoned to an obscure corner of the fishing vest or tackle box. Not that the Flatfish is not a fine lure, for it certainly is, and so are many others that enjoy brief local reputations. However, my night-fishing records and the records of many other anglers do prove that the serious night fly fisherman using standard night-fly patterns will outfish everyone else over the long haul.

TECHNIQUE

The basic principles of fly casting remain fairly constant. In applying these principles, each fisherman gradually evolves his own style of presentation. Any one of five competent fly rodders will perform each minute move in a way somewhat different from each of the other fellows. Fishing the night fly, or any fly, for that matter, soon gets to be a very personal thing. In discussing technique, all I can do is describe the methods that have worked for me and for a few other fishermen with whom I have been privileged to fish. As I mentioned before, the classic setup for the night fly fisherman is the moving lip of water at the tail end of a substantial pool. If you are familiar with the water you intend to fish, you will know about where the trout's night-time feeding position will be. It will be exactly where he lies in wait for the struggling mayflies to drift by. A big trout may be diverted from his special watching place to chase a minnow or some other creature, but he can be counted on to eventually return. In ninety percent of most night-fishing situations, the flies should be cast ten to twelve feet upstream from the trout's position. They should ride just below the surface and reach the beginning of their swing right in front of his nose. Bear in mind that we're discussing the ideal presentation. In practice, it can't always be so perfect. Now, if the fly pattern and size look right and if the speed of the drift appeals to him, the trout will rise up a bit from the bottom, and the battle will begin.

You and I both know that fishing is rarely quite that easy. Thousands of casts may be made before this perfect combination of events occurs. The drift may be too fast, the pattern and size may not be right, the fly silhouette may not be properly presented to the trout, and heaven only knows how many other things could go wrong. If you know for sure that the trout is in a given position — if he has, for example, shown himself to you by a false start for your flies or by a rise to some surface food — stick with him until you take him or until you're sure you have frightened him or you see another, larger fish show himself. Like the salmon, a large trout may refuse the same fly for fifty casts and suddenly, on the fifty-first, take it with a smashing strike. Or perhaps a change of pattern or size might do the trick.

The wisdom of using a dropper fly becomes apparent when you use this natural-drift technique. The flies should be at least twenty-eight inches apart to offer a dual-speed presentation. That phrase may sound confusing. What it means is simply this — as the flies turn at the end of their swing, the lead fly starts moving a bit faster than the dropper. With three flies you have the advantage of a third pattern and a third speed of retrieve. Any more than three flies becomes a bit difficult to cast and can lead to hopeless entanglements.

There is an ideal current speed for this style of night fishing. It could be presented in miles per hour, but that would be meaningless to most anglers, including me. The perfect speed might best be described as that which would move a pair of flies on a seven-foot leader and a floating line downstream at a velocity that would keep the flies from sinking more than a foot below the surface. Try casting your big flies into moving current during the daytime and you'll quickly see how much current is required to do this. Using this technique as a beginning, you can then branch out into variations on the theme. If the current is a bit faster than ideal, make your cast somewhat further upstream. If the water velocity is slower, cast a bit closer to your hoped-for hotspot and retrieve your flies with a hand-twist motion. In still or very slow water some artificial motion must be supplied to give the fly a lifelike quality. Trout in very slack water can be the most fickle fish of all. At times the retrieve must be extremely slow, and at other times extremely fast. In most cases, however, the slower retrieve will be more productive.

There is another great advantage that comes with the use of one or two dropper flies. As the flies near the end of their swing, the "hand fly," the one nearest the rod, will occasionally rise from the water and dance enticingly along the surface. At times, this action will drive a trout crazy. When a strike is made to a dancing dropper, it's usually an earth-shaker. You're fast to a fish right now, and you know it. Among the serious students of the black art, much streamside discussion has revolved around where to place the dropper fly. Some dedicated night flyers have declared that, when using three flies, twenty-four inches should be the separating distance. Some place the dropper at twenty-eight to thirty inches and the hand fly fifteen inches away, and so on and so on. The exact placement of the dropper probably depends more on the water you're fishing than on any other single factor. If the water is moving quite rapidly, the dropper should be a bit further back toward the rod. In very large streams, flies may be separated by thirty inches in an attempt to cover more water. It follows that on smaller streams that droppers should be a bit closer together.

All things considered, the prime advantage of using droppers is that it allows trout to have a look at more than one pattern. Salmon fishermen might recoil at the idea, but I think there is a place for using a dropper on Canadian streams where the usual fish is a four-to-five pound grilse. I mention this weight limit only because I have experienced the thrill of simultaneously hooking two fairly large trout at night. I have hooked enough doubleheaders to be quite sure of one's odds of landing both fish. Its a tough proposition, since the fish usually work against each other. The larger pulls the smaller, and the added pressure on the hook will cause it to tear out. When the fish are about the same size, the pull is equalized and the fisherman can sometimes simply stand there and let the two combatants slug it out until they tire. I caught two three-pounders one night, and the fight was no more spectacular than landing a soggy bath towel. The rod hardly flexed, though the two browns chose to do battle in deep water. They pulled and tugged for about three minutes and then allowed themselves to be skidded onto a gravel bar. With most doubleheaders the strikes do not occur simultaneously. The first fish causes the free fly to be jerked through the water in a manner that entices the second to strike. It just happens, and suddenly there are two disturbances on the surface when there should be only one.

Not only does the dropper allow the fisherman to show the fish two different patterns, it also gives him the opportunity to offer different sizes. As in daytime fishing, this size factor is usually important. It often has to do with the size of the food that's prevalent on that occasion, but it just as often has no connection whatever. One night on Kettle Creek, the trout were feeding with abandon on a "fall" (you couldn't call it a hatch) of ladybugs. To intelligently suggest this rather small insect we would have needed imitations tied on size-18 hooks. We knew the ladybugs were there because we saw them before it became completely dark. The trout were taking before dark, and they continued right on into the black hours. We tried a lot of small stuff before it became too dark to see them float. We then went through our boxes, looking for something smallish that would work as a nighttime seducer. Several 14s and 16s were tried but with no luck. Finally we went to the tried-and-true night-fly patterns of that particular season and immediately began to catch fish. As I recall, the patterns used were Hardy's Favorite and the New Page, which are hardly good suggestions of a ladybug but which were effective nevertheless. These were number-6 hooks, by the way.

I can recall many times when I've had a number 6 on the head position and a number 10 or smaller on as a dropper, and the smaller fly gathered all the strikes. And in an equal number of cases, the reverse has been true. I still prefer 6s as the most useful night-fly size, with 8s a close second.

I have at times used two flies of the same size and pattern on a cast, and the results can make it worthwhile. The late Eddie Cauffield, of Roulette, Pennsylvania, once proved to me most dramatically the wisdom of using a dropper fly of the same pattern as the lead fly. An enormous trout was fanning the shallow tailwater of the Goodsell Hole one evening, and since he was in a position that was especially vulnerable to drag, we decided not to try for him until dark. It must be understood that in our cult it was considered right and proper that a big trout should be fished for with night flies if at all possible. In the vernacular of today, "It was our thing." Eddie won the toss and would fish for him first. He was still rigged up from the night before, with a pair of Professors, size 6. I noted this and asked him if he were going to change one of them. He didn't change, remarking that if one Professor was good, two might be even better. I wish I could make the story more dramatic — something like how he succeeded after fifty casts or some such business — but it actually happened on the first cast. The head fly swung past the fish, which made a false start but didn't take. The dropper passed over him a second later, and he grabbed it. A good solid run, one leap, five minutes of thrashing around, and five pounds of brown trout lay flopping on the bank. The point here is that the dropper was used more for a change of presentation than for an alternate pattern. Both factors are important, but that *different look at the fly* is what frequently makes the difference.

THE APPROACH
AND THE CAST

While there are certain day-time fly-fishing approaches that will work at night, the methods that work best for the after-dark angler will be considerably different. The ideal arrangement includes ample time for the thoughtful fisherman to spend some daylight hours studying the pool or pools that he intends to fish that evening. Big trout on the prowl at night do not lie in the same places that they frequent during the sunlit period. They learned long ago that to survive means to stay out of sight when the water is low and not to venture into the shallows even when the water is at a normal height. Trout that have predominately become night feeders very closely adhere to this behavior pattern. *Where* you cast from is often the primary consideration if one is to catch many trout at night. Where you cast from determines the sort of "look" that the fish will give your fly or flies. If the look satisfies him and the pattern suits his fancy at the time, he's on! This business of giving the fish the right "look" at the fly is the foundation of Atlantic salmon fishing as well, and although I don't like to belabor the point, a good salmon fisherman should make a great night fisherman, and vice versa. The primary differences are in the location of the fish and in the speed of the strike.

To illustrate where and how to fish certain types of pools at night, this chapter includes some line drawings that show several basic pool formations. With minor variations, pools like these occur on practically every trout stream. It will readily be seen that the best position for the night angler is considerably different from the spot that the daytime tosser of floating flies would establish as home plate. In most cases, the dry fly must float unencumbered by drag, so the angler must be behind or to one side of his cast if many fish are to be hooked. A downstream cast is a most difficult method for hooking a fish that is taking naturals with the head-and-tail rise that most heavily feeding trout employ. The point of the hook is then headed in exactly the wrong direction. With wet flies, the trout turns his head as he strikes, giving the angler a better chance to hook him in the corner of the mouth. This is where seventy-five percent of fly-caught fish are hooked. This is even more the case with flies smaller than size 10. But the wider gap and large bend of the night-fly hook causes the fly to roll a bit higher on the normal strike and to hook the fish a little bit forward of the mouth corner. This is a good solid hold. Barring tackle failure, most of the fish hooked at night will be landed.

Pool Number One is of a very common sort of configuration and is the very best kind for night-fly work. On the larger streams, such a pool will contain several worthwhile trout, and an entire evening can be spent there. On streams that would normally be called brooks, one or two good trout might reside there, and the fisherman would have to move on after causing a commotion. When the water drops a bit in the

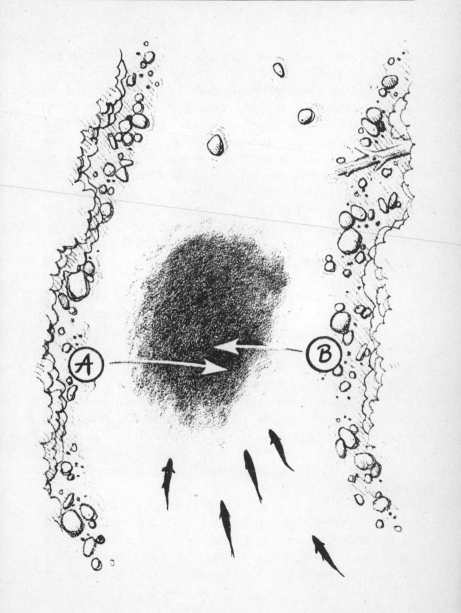

summer and the good evening rises commence, the fish will not remain in the darker patch of water. This is the deepest part of the pool, and to rise up from the bottom becomes too much of an effort. It is much easier for them to station themselves in the slick tailwater at the pool's exit and pick off the floating insects as they drift down the feeding channels. Some small trout will remain in the fast water at the very head of the pool, above the deep water. The big fellows prefer to have their noses pointed toward the escape route, which in this case means to deep water. This is the easiest place of all for the night fisherman, though it's frequently the hardest for the dry-fly caster. The increasing velocity of the slick water makes drag a problem, and a direct upstream cast usually lines the fish and spooks them completely. Positions A and B are equally good. The cast should be made into the edge of the black water and allowed to float freely across and down through the holding water. The fly will be presented to the fish in almost full profile, and this is the way he should see the pattern on the first cast. Little or no movement should be imparted to the fly for the first dozen casts. If a strike is not forthcoming, try a very slight hand-twist motion as the flies are sweeping through the arc. This should not be a violent jerk-jerk-jerk but rather a subtle undulating twist. Keep bigger fish in mind. They don't usually take with a wild rush but strike with a smooth, purposeful lunge that becomes their dignified size.

Whether to fish from position A or position B at the outset is a decision that may be made by your casting arm. If you are right-handed, position A is the obvious choice because your rod hand will be closer to the fish. After a half hour of casting from A with no luck, you may want to cross over and have a go at it from B. It just may work. The trout is a fickle fellow, and a reverse drift may be the subtle difference that proves to be his undoing.

At all night pools, if a fish is taken quickly (in the first six casts or so), go right back at it as soon as possible. The night feeding period may be over quickly, and the other fish in the pool may not have been startled in the least. If nothing more happens in the next dozen or so casts, reel in and rest the pool for fifteen minutes. On some nights trout are very nervous about unnatural splashing. On others they couldn't care less, or seem to be attracted to it. I'm sure that most of you dry-fly fishermen have been in the midst of hatches when trout were jumping right beside your boot tops. You know damned well they see you, but they just don't seem to mind. On the next evening, a puff of smoke from your pipe will send them dashing for cover.

Pool Number Two is also a common setup. Overhanging branches allow cover, and as this is a shallow area, the current will be somewhat slower. The water is shallowest on side A, and only a very foolish trout would take up a feeding station there, day or night. Some very small ones may be foolish enough to do so, but since most fishermen will pound this side of the pool, the larger trout will seldom take a stand there. They will stay close to the dark holding water on side B, and because an occasional bite of food in the form of measuring worms or other tree-borne creatures might be available, this is where they'll be at night.

The tendency is strong to fish from A, and though it may work, the flies will probably sweep through the prime water with too much speed to be attractive. B is the best spot from which to cast. There you have the advantage of casting from a

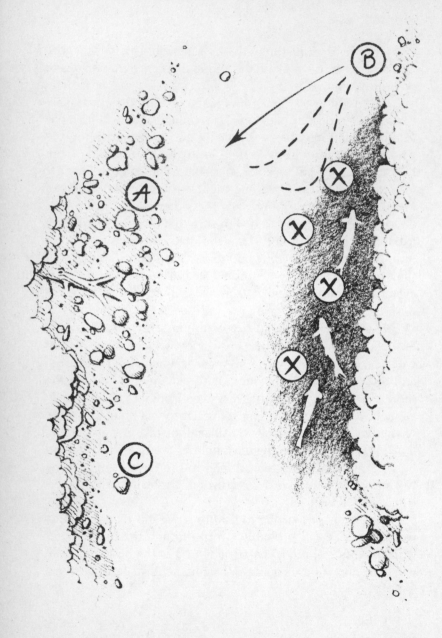

concealed position, although you must contend with having to bring the flies back through the hot spot to prepare for the next cast. Most strikes will occur at the spots marked with an X. The flies will be swinging into the fish's observation window from the deep-water side. If inclined to take, the trout will probably strike at them just before they hang directly in front of him. If he waits until they are hanging "dead" in a direct downstream attitude, you'll have a devil of a time hooking him. The direct downstream strike is the most difficult, and though it is hard to remember, there is a way to overcome this handicap. Allow a six-inch loop of line to drop between the fingers of your rod hand. This loop serves as a shock absorber and allows the fish to take the fly a few inches before he feels the resistance of the rod tip. If the line is straight out, the pull will be sudden, and if you don't miss your fish altogether, the chances are you'll hook him very lightly on the tip of the snoot or lower lip. Glenn Shaw showed me this trick forty-three years ago, when I was ten years old, and I've been indebted to him ever since.

You can fish this sort of pool from position A if you cannot wade across or for some other reason can't get to B. Alternate position C is not bad. It gives the fisherman a chance to present the fish with a different "look" at the flies. To do this right, however, requires a rather quick take-up of slack line, to avoid loss of line control. The fish will not have a long look at the flies, unless you can cast a fancy button hook into your line. A situation like this presents a good argument for a long fly rod. Although I have no quarrel with those who prefer the short midge- and flea-type rods, such gear just cannot do as good a job of swimming the larger night flies as do the longer sticks. I like an eight-foot rod for most night work, and there are times when a nine-footer is not out of place. This situation is one of them. With a long rod the line can be held above the central part of the current and the flies can be "tickled" through the hot spot.

Pool Number Three is another ideal situation for night flies. The dark, deep, hiding water is on the left side of the stream, and an undercut bank is a typical configuration in pools of this sort. The trout will drift out into the quieter water during the evening hours, and the dry-fly man will get a crack at them here, too. The current will want to pull the flies toward the undercut bank, and this works to the angler's advantage. The flies are usually presented to the fish in a profile attitude that gives him a good look at the patterns. Start with a very short cast aimed at right angles to the current. Gradually lengthen the line while at the same time casting further upstream. The fish may be very close to the edge of the black water, or they may drift a considerable distance away from it. If there has been a good evening hatch, chances are that the fish have strayed further than usual from the bank. A dead drift is best in this situation, but if no strikes come after a good trial period, try a bit of hand-twist retrieving. Even on small streams, these undercut-bank pools can contain large numbers of trout. Frequently a big one will be lurking there. It is always a good bet, day or night, to approach undercut pools from downstream. For some reason, trout in positions like this are especially watchful of floating or rolling debris. In clear water they can be very spooky, even at night. Unless the pool is an especially large one, the trout hooked in a pool like this will seldom be lost. They have one thing in mind after being struck, and that is to seek escape by pulling strongly to one side, heading for the protective overhang of the bank and

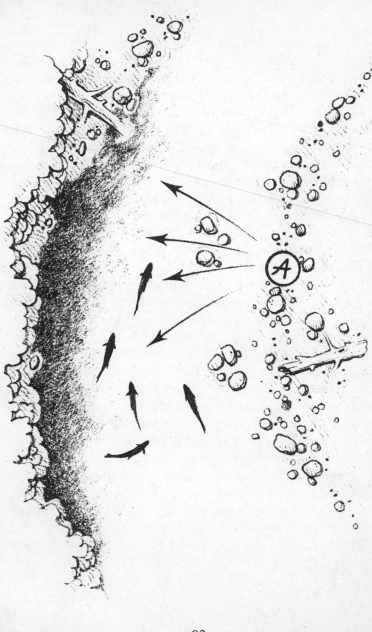

the roots and other obstacles that gather in such locations. The steady sideways pull combined with the flow of the current will prevent a twisting motion of the hook or a change in position that can work a big hook loose.

I believe this business of hook size is an extremely relevant matter. The dry-fly fisherman will argue, with considerable merit, that a small hook — number 14 or smaller — will bite in more securely than a larger one. This is true up to a point. The very small-size hooks, 16s through 24s, sometimes bury themselves in a trout's jaw. After that, you can hardly lose him if the leader doesn't break. On trout over 18 inches, a hook in the 6 to 10 range will attach itself with authority, but if the hook is larger, it will have a tendency to tear a large hole during a prolonged fight.

Pool Number Four. A large obstruction in the center of the pool can sometimes create a special holding place for trout that is a delight for the dry-fly fisherman. When a good hatch is in progress he can work his way around the rock or log or whatever formed the pool and can pick up trout with impunity. It can be a tough post for the night fisherman because the trout will usually move to the lower edge of the calm water, just before the point where the water speeds up over the lip of the pool. This is a favorite night gathering position for big trout, and the night fisherman should always keep this in mind. If the trout hang too close to fast exit water, they can be tough to entice. The flies gain momentum at exactly the wrong time, and your chances are blown. There is a pool, almost precisely like the one in the drawing, on Pine Creek that had me perplexed for a long time. The trout there still do not cooperate all the time, but I now manage to take at least one fish there almost every night that they are in a striking mood.

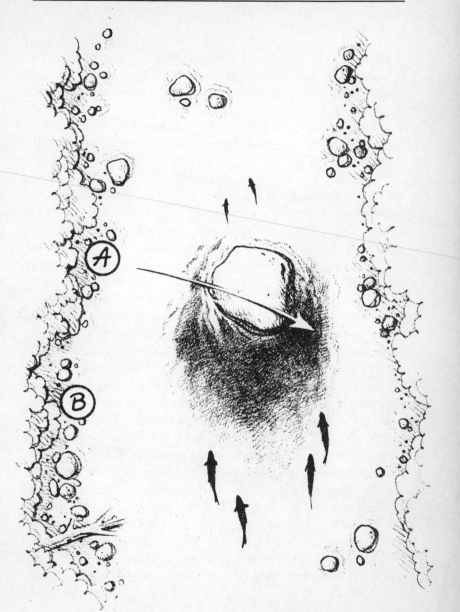

My problem was that I always made my first effort from position B, since I usually approached the pool from the downstream direction. It was simply more convenient because this pool was immediately above my favorite pool on this particular stretch, and I usually didn't give it my attention until after I'd been fishing for a while. It seemed as though B was the place from which to cast, but only on rare occasions could I raise a fish. I had seen some real monsters scooting around in the shallows, but five minutes of casting would put them down. In working upstream, I would invariably move to A and fish for the trout that were occasionally feeding just ahead of the holding water and, just as invariably, would hook a small trout. The distance from B to A was not more than twelve feet. On one perfect evening — there had been a beautiful, rosy sunset — I dallied longer than usual at A. I had caught not one but two little fellows at the head of the rock when a mighty trout made a huge swirl at the tail end of the pool and then made a splash that sounded like a watermelon thrown into the stream. For some reason I did not move back to B, which would have been the normal thing to do, but instead checked my upstream cast in midair, changed direction, and cast right over the top of the boulder. The current on the far side of the boulder moved a bit faster than it did on my side, a fact that I had not discovered until just then. (Actually, I wasn't absolutely certain of this until the next week when I scouted the pool during the day.) My flies, instead of being sucked out of the slow water and into the fast, as always happened when casting from B, instead rode along at a rather steady pace. The "look" that was offered must have been right. A broad-shouldered brown trout of twenty-five inches seized the dropper on the first cast and in one surge of power darted to the far side of the boulder and proceeded to saw my line on the sharp edges. I raced from A down to the tail of the pool and began to pump and reel, saltwater fashion, to bring him out from under the rock. This rather crude technique, which is not recommended for use with 6X leaders, brought him near the top, where a lot of wild thrashing took place, but never once did he make an honest-to-goodness jump. A few minutes later I beached one of the most beautiful brown trout I've ever seen.

I rested the pool for ten minutes, then hooked a trout of nearly eighteen inches by pulling the same stunt of casting right across the boulder and allowing the line to slip down over it. This fish was returned after a battle that included four tail-spinning jumps. I called it a night after that performance and walked the half mile back to the car with a big smile and a big trout.

Pool Number Five is another prime night-fishing location. When summer temperatures put the main stream up into the uncomfortable range, trout will congregate in the cool fan of water that is created where a small brook enters the main-stream. The configuration of this sort of setup varies consider-ably, but the example shown is typical. The tendency is strong to fish from either A or B. This is where the bait fishermen set their little "Y" sticks for holding the rod after tossing a gob of nightcrawlers out into the black water. They will do right well, too, under early summer conditions. When night-feeding time approaches, the fish will ease up into the blended current, keeping an eye on floating matter coming down the main stream while watching the side stream as well. They are there for food and comfort. At B or A the angler is usually too close to the fish, and even worse, the flies usually cannot be well

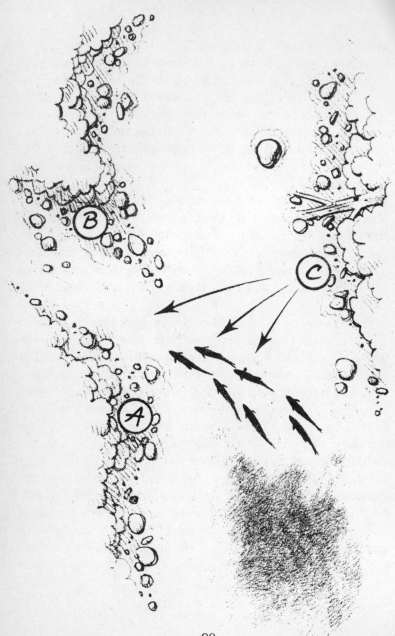

presented from either place. Even though B looks like an excellent choice and may produce some strikes, you are faced there with that problem of casting directly downstream. This makes the fish cussedly tough to hook, and one is about all you'll get before spooking the whole assembly, and an assembly is just what you may find at such a spot. There are certain spring runs that draw dozens of trout at night. With the aid of a flashlight, I have seen a hundred or more big fish lying bumper to bumper on a hot August night at such locations, and this on a hard-fished eastern stream.

The spot to fish from is C. Cast from the bank if you can, though some cautious wading here should not cause any problems. The current that holds the trouts' attention is the one coming from the side stream, so any debris that you stir up will drift away out of their line of sight. By gradually lengthening successive casts, the angler can methodically work over this location. Fish hooked in these feeder-stream locations almost always turn and run downstream. Thus, each fish hooked can be fought and landed well away from the hotspot, and if the fish continue to strike, the night angler can do a land-office business. I was with Pinney at such a spot one night when he hooked eleven trout without moving out of his tracks. Several of them were sixteen inches or better. I was standing almost beside him and caught five more.

The best part about these little side streams is that once you locate a productive one, you can fish it every night. New and different trout will be moving into the cool water each night, and the supply never seems to run out, though it will, of course, if you kill every trout you catch. Even we greedy night flyers don't do that. After all, how many twenty-inch trout can one man eat? Naturally, I'm joking, since no one, at least no one that I know, catches twenty-inch trout with any regularity on trout streams anywhere in the United States. But we could if more fifteen-inchers were put back to grow just a bit more. This is particularly true of brown trout.

Any pool that the stream fisherman will encounter can be roughly classed in one of the foregoing five categories. It will take a little imagination to adapt one's personal techniques to the pools on his favorite stream. But imagination is a commodity that most trout fishermen have an abundance of, and the night fisherman must have it if he is to be successful. The important thing to remember is to give the fish a look at the side of the flies rather than an end-on view. Unlike the dry fly, in which the silhouette is the most important factor, the wet fly is viewed in its entirety, or should be. If pattern were not important in fly fishing, we would have no need for different colored hackles, body materials, and wings. We could simply tie all of our flies in a neutral gray and forget all about color. But, what a lot of good conversation would be lost.

It would have served no purpose to illustrate a flat expanse of still or very gently moving water. Long, flat stretches of river or quiet pond water require the fisherman to move his flies in some manner in order to drum up a strike. The hand-twist retrieve is a good way to start in quiet water. One can fish very close to the surface by using an ordinary dry-fly line, or he can choose to go much deeper with a sinking or sink-tip line. During the past three seasons, I have been doing more and more fishing at night with a sink-tip line, and I find it to be just the ticket for ponds and some of the larger rivers. On some streams, however, the sink-tip pulls the flies too close to the bottom, and a dead sort of action is the result. But on ponds the sink-tip is ideal. Unless the flies must sink down ten feet or more, most fishermen will find the sink-tip easier to manage than a complete sinker. It is much easier to pick up for the next cast. Although I like the total sinker for certain purposes, it is an abomination to pick up gracefully. It cannot be picked up like a floater but must be pulled free of the water, putting a taxing strain on a good bamboo rod. I would never use a sinking fly line on a bamboo rod that I cared much about. The casting of heavy lines and flies will sap the strength of a bamboo stick faster than the catching of a hundred big trout.

Before closing this section, I have to mention the riffle hitch, or as some choose to call it, the Portland hitch. Salmon fishermen have been using it for some time, and it has certainly proved its worth in late summer and fall fishing for Atlantics. Charlie Fox showed it to me one night on his famous section of the Letort. I was engaged in casting a pair of night flies at a particularly big fish that was making huge wakes as it cruised about the Buttonwood pool. "Did you ever try the riffle hitch at night?" Charlie asked. No, I hadn't...had he? No, but it certainly worked on recalcitrant salmon.

"How do you make the riffle hitch?"

"Simply take a half hitch around the head of the fly, snug it up, and that's all there is to it." Sounded simple enough. It would make a great story if I had succeeded in catching that particular trout with a riffle hitch. I didn't, but I did take one two nights later by looping my leader around the fly. Since that night five years ago, I have taken many trout by the use of the extra half hitch, and I recommend it highly for still or very glassy water. The idea is to keep the fly planing along on top of the water with the hook bend at right angles to the flow of the current. What it does, actually, is to give the fish a look at the fly that he couldn't possibly have if the fly were attached in the ordinary manner.

You may have guessed another application of the riffle hitch: when the night fly fisherman is faced with the necessity of casting directly downstream at a good fish. As I've said before, these fish are among the most difficult to hook, but with the riffle hitch the hook point is at right angles to the trout's mouth and, as a bonus, he can see the entire fly, and this makes a difference too. When he hits, he takes the fly crosswise in his mouth, and the strike puts the fly right where it should go — into the corner of the jaw. I've taken several dozen trout at night using the rifle hitch, and that's where most of them have been hooked.

It isn't necessary to attach the dropper or hand fly with a riffle hitch because they are flopping around rather freely. The point fly is the one that should be attached this way, and sometimes a single fly with this arrangement is better than a dual rig. The idea is to bring the fly across the surface like a little surfboard and to keep it on the surface, or rather, in the surface. There is a fine distinction here. In the surface is a better expression. Give it a try. It's an effective way to fish ponds or still pools when orthodox procedures fail to produce. I should point out that the strike to a riffle-hitched fly is usually violent. You will have no trouble setting the hook.

BOB PINNEY —
NIGHT FISHERMAN

The trout was the master that Robert N. Pinney was born to serve. Lesser gods in his special religion were the ruffed grouse and the wild turkey. When he could not be in active pursuit of one of these, he consoled himself by reading about them. Until 1963, the year of his death, there was scarcely a published title that involved hunting or fishing that didn't come under his careful scrutiny, and when I say careful, I really mean it. When Bob read a book and liked it, he would reread and study it until he could recall whole chapters nearly verbatim. He memorized almost entirely Skue's *The Way of a Trout With a Fly*. Hewitt and La Branche were most familiar to him and so were such moderns as Flick, Fox, and Schwiebert. Most of these fishing writers have much to say about dry-fly fishing, but Bob was enough of a scholar to apply their observations to his specialty of swimming the big night flies through northern Allegheny waters. Not that he didn't fish with the dry fly — he most certainly did, and more expertly than most of us can ever hope to duplicate. He knew more than a dozen streams so intimately that he seldom made a cast to any spot that did not hold a fish. Pinney was also one of the few fishermen that I know of who really could drum up a fish by "creating a hatch" with repeated casts. He could place his fly in exactly the same spot time after time until a curious fish could no longer stand the pressure. Incidentally, this is a most productive trick on small streams when no particular hatch is evident.

During the twenty-year period that I fished with Bob he worked as a night clerk at the local hotel, beginning his stint at the desk at midnight. It was an ideal job for one who liked to hunt and fish. He never married and lived with his mother until her death and, later, with his sister. For Bob, this was idyllic life, as it perhaps might be for many of us. He fished whenever he wanted to, which was every day the weather would permit during the open season. When arriving with others at a new spot, he was always the first to be ready and the last to reel up. To say that Pinney liked to fish would be an insult. He had to fish.

As much as he enjoyed fishing with the dry fly, the challenge of night fishing made him prefer this phase of angling to all others. In his more than fifty years of trout fishing he caught his fill of ten- and twelve-inchers; fifteen-inchers were commonplace to him; eighteen-inchers brought a muffled grunt of appreciation; two-footers . . . now that was what Pinney was after, and his lifetime total of brown trout over twenty inches must have numbered in the hundreds. I personally saw him catch several dozen over that mark, and these were taken from the often-referred-to "civilized waters of the East."

I was thirteen years old when I had my first encounter with Bob Pinney. Armed with a new pair of boots and some flies that I had tied, and fortified with all the knowledge that *Herter's Fly Tying Manual* and Ray Bergman's *Trout* could

offer, I journeyed to the Goodsell Hole on a beautiful June evening. This was Mecca for the fishermen of three counties and parts more distant. The Allegheny River and Mill Creek joined there, and for a century it was the greatest trout-producing pool in Pennsylvania and, for that matter, maybe for the entire eastern United States. A minor whirlpool of conflicting currents dominated the center of this hundred-foot circular trout factory. Goodsell's depth in the center was calculated to be about twenty feet. The smaller fish would frequently rise all day long in the eye of the pool, but it was only the most skillful caster who could take these fish with regularity. The pool changed slightly from year to year under the turbulence of ice chunks and melting snow-water, but during the ten-year period that I fished it, it was fairly constant in configuration. The broad lip of slick water that formed its tail was the most perfectly created night-fishing spot that I have ever seen. It was into this pool that I waded that night.

As usual, some rather smallish trout were rising in the pool's center, and it seemed to me that the best way to reach them was the direct approach of wading into the tail of the pool and casting directly upstream. I didn't wade as cautiously as I should have, and several heavy "V"s moving swiftly upstream told me that I had done something wrong. "If you want to catch any trout later on this evening, you'll have to stay out of the pool."

The voice was Pinney's. He was sitting toadlike on a drift-wood log about twelve feet back from the edge of the pool. I had seen the great one many times before. He would be walking home from the hotel while I was on my way to school in the morning. We had never spoken, but being perhaps the best fly fisherman in a community of fishermen makes one well known. I got out of the stream, since I knew that local custom indicated that Pinney was one of the caretakers of the Goodsell. He motioned for me to sit down beside him on the end of the log. That was the beginning of a fishing friendship that lasted twenty years. I would not trade a second of it for any other experience in the world.

For the first two years of our instructor-student relationship, the talk of fishing was mostly of dry flies and daylight fishing. As I grew older (and was allowed to stay out later at night), the heady thrill of feeling a heavy trout strike the big wet flies permanently retarded my growth as an all-round fisherman. Under Pinney's guidance, my thinking was shifted from creels full of pan-sized trout to the kind that are transported by two fingers through the gills. I managed to take enough big trout on night flies during my teenage years to establish a lifestyle that has since cost me many sleepless nights.

Pinney and a dozen others of equal or near-equal skill began night fishing for trout during the years of the First World War. The brown trout (rather unpopular at that time) had recently been introduced into northern Pennsylvania waters, and the dry fly was just becoming popular. The more resourceful anglers soon discovered that the brown was not quite so gullible as the native brookie, and fishing styles had to be altered. The usual downstream jiggle-and-jerk technique that worked so well with three small wets when the quarry was brook trout was not the best way to catch the sophisticated European. The smaller browns responded well enough to this style, but the larger browns just didn't buy it. More attention had to be spent on presentation of the bait or fly.

Tackle had to be changed also. The soft, extremely limber "buggy whip" rods that worked so well for the staandard wet-fly approach to the hordes of little speckled trout didn't hold up well under the increased false casting that was needed to keep the new dry flies floating. And if one was lucky enough to sink a hook into a king-sized brown, these rods didn't have the power to turn him. This brown-trout-dry-fly revolution affected the entire eastern United States, and since that was where most of the tackle buying took place, the rod makers reacted. In fact, they overreacted, and anglers were burdened with twenty years of rods that were too stiff for most purposes. A few skillful rod makers caught on and discovered that the ideal rod for dry-fly work had power next to the butt and a sensitive tip to protect the delicate leaders that dry-fly fishing required. The ideal night rod is the same kind of creature.

Pinney and his contemporaries learned, mostly from Doc Phillips, that the big browns would strike flies at night. Fly-fishing history would be made in northern Pennsylvania because of this discovery, though night fishing for trout and other species undoubtedly developed in other areas in much the same manner. At first, the experimenter used his favorite brook-trout wet-fly patterns in sizes 10, 12, and 14, and he caught some trout, but it was soon discovered that these "little" flies left something to be desired.

Incredibly, there were very few fly tiers among this early group of night flyers. They depended heavily on mail-order flies, probably because good materials were not generally available in the United States. The fast-becoming-popular dry fly was best obtained from England. Pinney and his friends bought hundreds of flies from Hardy, Cummins, and C. Farlow. In general, they were poor flies by today's standards, though much better than anything our tiers produced during the 20s and 30s. Also pictured in those magnificent

British catalogues were the larger loch and sea-trout flies. The Goodsell Hole devotees reasoned that since the sea trout of the British Isles were nothing other than migrant browns, the flies designed for them might do well on the transplanted browns. Some of the big flies that visiting anglers brought in from the brook trout regions of Maine and Canada also looked appealing, and they, too, were tried.

The period between World Wars One and Two constituted the halcyon years of night fly fishing in Pennsylvania, and for that matter in the entire East. A combination of factors brought this about. More anglers could afford automobiles, and this caused a branching out of angling talent and a widespread exchange of ideas. Unavoidably, the population increase was making itself felt on trout streams. This caused a few serious fishermen to begin retreating to the dark hours for the practice of their sport. Not a great many took to the streams at night, but enough to make their presence felt in the development of night fishing as a specific branch of trout angling.

I'm sure that it must sound a bit presumptuous for me to suggest that the history of night fly fishing in America revolved around one particular pool in a remote corner of northcentral Pennsylvania. Well, here goes, and I'm sure issue will be taken, for I am not only suggesting that here is where it all started, I'm flatly declaring it. Even on the famed brown-trout waters of the Catskills, where much angling history was made, night fishing for brown trout is still relatively in its infancy. There certainly are a few after-dark types probing the Willowemoc and the Neversink, but their number remains small indeed. Even along the fabled Letort and the much-revered Yellow Breeches in southcentral Pennsylvania, this business of fishing for trout after dark had no sound base until

1953. And here lies a short story.

Gene Utech, of Gettysburg, Pennsylvania, was working for the Department of Highways during the summer of 1953. As a member of a traffic survey crew, he found himself in Coudersport on a warm June evening. His party would be there the balance of the summer. The people who decide such things announced that the crew would make the Crittenden Hotel their sleeping headquarters. Gene was a fly fisherman, and since Bob Pinney was the night clerk at the hotel, it was just a matter of time until they would fish together. (Gene was a fly tier and a serious student of angling, and Pinney was hard-pressed for flies. His favorite fly tier was not available, since a thing called the Korean War was then in progress and the tier's friends and neighbors thought that his talents were needed in places other than on a log beside a trout stream.)

Utech was a good student. He absorbed as much night-fishing lore and technique from Pinney in one season as is humanly possible, and he realized very quickly that here was a live fishing legend. Tragically, the Goodsell ceased to exist the next summer. The Coudersport city fathers, with considerable urging from the United States Corps of Engineers, decided to construct a concrete flood-control channel through the center of town. There would have been other, far cheaper ways to handle the occasional flash flood that hit the Allegheny Mountains, but the Corps, in its doubtful wisdom, elected to do it the hard way. The Goodsell Hole and the other excellent pools that lay within the city limits became nothing more than concrete hog troughs. In a way it's a good thing that I wasn't in Coudersport when the construction was going on. If I had been, I would probably be writing these pages from the confines of a Leavenworth cell.

But there were other good night-fishing pools, and Pinney introduced Utech to many of them. This story would be no different from a thousand other chance meetings of two fishermen, except for one significant factor: Returning to the limestone streams of Cumberland County, Utech brought with him a bundle of night-fishing theory. After sitting at the right hand of the master for a full season, he wasn't overly surprised to discover that a big fuzzy Governor and a handsome Professor presented at night would fool the sophisticated limestone trout as easily as they would their northern cousins.

There had been a few isolated attempts at night fishing in the Cumberland County region before Utech's initial forays, but not with the big wets that I consider to be "night flies." The general line of thinking in the limestone country was oriented toward daytime fishing. Fly fishing there meant smallish flies, fine leaders, and cautious casts. The act of dunking a pair of number 6s was considered almost barbaric by the cadre of fly fishermen headed by the famous Fox-Marinaro coalition.

In the winter of 1964 I packed my rods, shotguns, and family and moved to Camp Hill, Pennsylvania. The fact that the Letort and many other limestone streams were but a twenty-minute drive from this suburban Harrisburg community played no small part in my decision to accept a job as associate editor of the *Pennsylvania Game News*. I would at last have a chance to prove or disprove to my own satisfaction that this special breed of surface-feeding brown trout would respond to the big flies after dark.

They did, indeed, but there were certain differences. Those of us who had spent most of our adolescent and adult years pursuing the black art of night fishing were convinced that water temperature was a critical factor in the overall picture. Water temperature is important in all types of fishing, but I have become convinced that night-feeding trout are especially sensitive to it and are frequently triggered into a feeding attitude by the change of a single degree, up or down. The limestone streams have as their sources the deeply rooted springs that bubble up from faults in the limestone structures peculiar to the valleys of the southcentral Appalachians. The surface temperatures of these waters do not fluctuate as abruptly as they do on the more rapidly flowing freestone waters of other parts of the United States. Once a desirable temperature occurs the freestone trout will feed long into the night before some other outside condition triggers the halt. Because of the more constant average water temperatures in the limestone streams, the night-feeding period is a very short one.

Letort trout, for instance, will operate as night-feeders for about an hour or hour and a half immediately after total darkness. Because of the abundance of underwater food (sow bugs, freshwater shrimp, crayfish, etc.) the big browns feed quickly and apparently get their fill rather soon. They have no need to feed long into the night, and as a rule they don't. But that first hour and a half are terrific. A pair of size 10s, or perhaps 8s at odd times, will work. The limestone trout especially like combinations of pink and orange. The old Yellow Dun is a good one, and so are the Queen of Waters, the Gold Ribbed Pink Lady, and Hardy's Favorite. The *Ephemerellas* are present after dark, so slightly smaller flies work somewhat better. These snooty fish may not look at a dry that is not tied onto a 6X tippet during the daytime, but they will freely take a wet on a chunk of six-pound test at night. The daytime angler benefits from this cooler water, as evidenced by the willingness of limestone trout to rise during the heat of the day in July and August. During the dog days of summer, midday fishing on most freestone streams in the United States is an exercise in futility.

The bountiful assortment of mayflies that inhabit the freestone streams is not available to the limestone trout. With the exception of some of the larger *Hexagenias*, most of the limestone mayflies are rather small, with the most important being the Pale Sulfur. For this reason, the general make-up of limestone night flies has to be a bit different from those that produce well in most other parts of the country. There is much experimenting yet to be done here.

In all areas where much night flying has been done, there is one ingredient that has a universal appeal — peacock herl. I have yet to find night-feeding fish in any part of the world that won't accept a fly tied with a peacock-herl body. For that matter, fish, anywhere, at any time, can be caught on peacock herl. I'm sure that this material would be used a lot more than it is for saltwater flies if it were not for the fragility of the quill. All peacock-herl bodies should be reinforced with fine gold wire or thread. I mention this because the old-fashioned Governor (red tip) and the Lead Wing Coachman seem to do as well as anything on limestone waters. In fact, the Governor catches fish just about everywhere. To date, I have taken trout, salmon, bass, and assorted panfish on the Governor in at least fifteen eastern and western states. Of course, I tie one on quite often, and that just may have something to do with it.

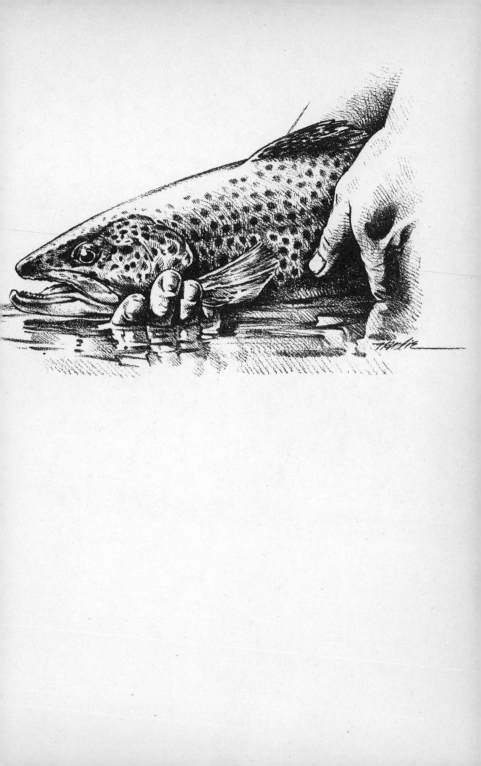

SOME LOOSE ENDS

A night fisherman learns to roll with the verbal punches that are thrown his way. His sanity is frequently questioned when his neighbors watch him stow tackle in the car and drive away at 10:30 or 11:00 in the evening. Daytime fishermen who proclaim that it's time to quit when they can no longer see the fly even murmur such remarks as "unsporting," "not civilized," and "no fun horsing them out on those big flies." The night fisherman must learn to be tough-skinned and to go about his business with all the panache he can muster. He knows things that they do not. For example: Tonight the moon will set at 10:25 and things will start happening (if they're going to happen) shortly thereafter.

Ah, the moon! That's the magic ingredient we haven't mentioned yet. Perhaps at times the largemouth bass leaps at the moon, but in my experience the brown trout and most other game fish do not. I have never caught a sizeable brown trout on a bright moonlit night. I have never seen one caught on such a night. Some trout are caught on bright nights, to be sure, but the really finest nights of all are the coal-black ones that are prefaced by a beautiful sunset.

The days that offer some good early evening activity on dry

flies sometimes lead into excellent night fly fishing. This is especially true when the "hatch" is really a fall of good-sized spinners. During the beautiful dance of mayflies, the trout have not had much of a chance to have a go at them. Then, as the night wears on, the spinners complete their egg laying and fall to the water. Now they can be easily slurped up by night-feeding trout, and this situation may offer some outstanding night fishing — and then again, it may not. The problem is often in the very number of flies available. The same excess of naturals sometimes plagues the daytime angler. The numbers of duns or spinners present may be so great that the fish have very little chance of finding an imitation in the welter of naturals. At night, the odds are probably even greater. If the right quantity of spinners is present, the night fly may do a rushing business.

But the moon should be in the right place. And just where is that? After thirty-nine years of night-fishing experience, I'm still not exactly sure. On nights when the moon is rising, I've done my best fishing about a half hour before it peers over the nearest hill. If the moon is present when I arrive at the stream, I really don't expect to do much until it has been out of sight for a half hour. Before any reader decides that Pinney may have influenced me too much, let me be quick to add that I've stayed on and fished in the bright moonlight many times. The night was often so perfect otherwise that it seemed inevitable that the fish would take — but they didn't.

And what does a pretty sunset have to do with it? Again, I'm not too sure, but perhaps it's an indication of a rather steady barometer. An evening that is glowering with storm clouds is usually not a productive one, unless the storm is to be one of the quick summer varieties that pass through in an hour or less. If the barometer rises quickly after the rain passes, a sudden summer shower can bring a wild feeding period. The bait fisherman knows this, and he'll be on the stream in an instant if the water becomes slightly discolored. The fly fisherman doesn't want cloudy water, but if it hasn't rained quite enough to cloud the water, he may do some business.

The day after Memorial Day, 1957, was unusually warm and cloudless. It was just the right kind of day for a sudden cold front to sweep in and create a crashing thunderstorm. That's exactly what happened. The storm hit about 6:30 p.m. and lasted no longer than twenty minutes. The air temperature dropped from about 80 to 65 degrees within two hours after the storm. There was a rather interesting purple sunset, and on the far horizon a few traces of lightning were still flickering. I didn't especially like the idea of going fishing while lightning was still evident, but the colorful sunset seemed to point to good fishing. Nothing happened until about ten o'clock, when the lightning started to come closer. There were a few flies hatching, and the odd fish was rising now and then, but I hadn't had a single strike. In an instant, the sky became cloudy and a light rain began to fall. The rain seemed warmer than the air temperature, and I was tempted to quit, when BANG! the rod was throbbing in my hand and I was fast to a really good fish. A run of over 60 feet was the trout's first stunt. This was followed by a couple of powerful leaps. From then on, it was a bitter tug of war until I slid the fish up a gently sloping sandbar. The trout was twenty-one-inches long and later proved to weigh nearly five pounds — a very healthy brown trout! The outstanding fight was the result of hook placement. The fish had been hooked in the back, just ahead of the adipose fin. I was happy about landing him but not as delighted as I would have been had the fish been fairly hooked in the jaw. A fluke, I thought. May as well go home. Besides, it's raining harder than ever. Oh, well, one more cast won't hurt anything. I'm well-soaked anyway.

I hooked and landed seven more fish in less than an hour and felt at least five more hard strikes. The shortest of the lot was sixteen inches, and the largest was a half inch longer than the first one. I took almost eighteen pounds of fish from civilized waters in one evening! It was the best single-night's catch I've ever made from Pennsylvania waters. I remember the flies I used. (How could I forget?) They were a number-6 Hardy's Favorite and that old standby, the Professor. I think the Professor was a number 8.

The action ceased as abruptly as it had begun. The switch was snapped. This is a fairly common experience in angling, but it seems to occur with particularly dramatic impact in fly fishing, and especially in night fly fishing. I can recall dozens of instances in which something suddenly triggered the fish into a feeding session and just as suddenly turned them off. When a sudden hatch of aquatic insects appears, the reason for these feeding orgies seems obvious. But is it? On similar evenings with a like amount of surface food available the trout may begin to feed at totally different times, or they may not feed at all.

A few years ago a fishing writer came up with the imaginative suggestion that the very best way to take selective trout is to fish with the nymph imitation of the fly that is scheduled to hatch next, instead of the dun or spinner imitation of the fly that is on the water now. In fact, he claimed to have tested his theory at some length and found it was positively deadly. It's a grand idea, but I can't believe that a trout would go poking around the bottom looking for the nymph of next week's selection when this week's menu is readily available. I don't think that the trout cares a whit if his next mouthful is an adult *Stenonema vicarium* or a nymphal *Stenonema ithaca*.

The amount of food available is surely a factor in determining when fish will feed, at night or at anytime. The barometer is certainly important, and so, I believe, is the moon. All of these variables are tied in a rather complex fashion to the water temperature, which is probably the single most important condition a night fly fisherman should consider. What, then, is the perfect combination?

My fishing diary indicates that the perfect night for tossing the big flies is dark with no moon at all. The air temperature should be about 70 degrees, the water temperature five degrees cooler. There should have been some surface activity before final darkness establishes itself, and there should also have been a stunning sunset. A very mild westerly breeze (just a skiff, mind you) should be blowing. I'll admit that these conditions seldom coexist, but if you do happen to be fishing on an evening when they do and you don't catch at least one fish after dark, you are a marked man and should seek a new form of recreation.

You may also be a marked man if your first serious night-fishing adventure includes a solid strike and the surge of a respectable trout. If the mystery of why the trout seized your fly continues to fascinate you, and you return to the river again to seek the answer, you may well have gone over the brink. In which case, welcome to the sublime foolishness of the night-fishing game.

SOME FAVORITE NIGHT FLY PATTERNS

Alexandria. There are many standard ways to tie this old British favorite. The dressing that has proved best for me consists of red hackle-wisp tail, embossed silver tinsel body, peacock sword feather wing (tied full — at least a dozen barbules), and black hackle tied in beard fashion. Size 8.

Female Beaverkill. This was once a favorite of the daytime wet-fly fisherman and was used with great success. It's not seen much these days, but some good night catches have been made with it. Slate duck wing, gray dubbing body with yellow chenille butt and brown hackle. The idea is to suggest the female Hendrickson. Sizes 8 and 10.

Black June. Another black fly that has the advantage of a peacock-herl body. Tied like the Black Prince except for the body.

Black Prince. There are many black flies that probably do as well, but the Prince has always been my favorite. Black tail, black silk body ribbed with silver, black duck secondary wing, and black hackle. I don't often tie on a black fly, but when the fish decide that black is on the menu, nothing else will do as well. The body should be well built up with wool or chenille before the silk is wound on. This presents a fatter look without requiring so many wraps of floss. Sizes 8 and 10.

Brown Hackle and Brown Palmer. The same effect is given by both these patterns, and by changing the body color, you wind up with Brown Hackle Red, Brown Hackle Yellow, or whatever. If the palmer tie is wanted, wind the hackle in at the tail (tip end first) and wrap it forward. A big, fully tied Brown Palmer with a red body has worked well for me on occasion, and I understand that the New Zealand anglers like it. They do a lot of night fishing for big browns over there, and red is a popular color with fish and fishermen.

Light Cahill. This extremely popular dry fly can do a good job at night during the early summer. Tie it full and "meaty" with an extra-thick body of cream fox fur. Light straw hackle and wood duck wings and tail. Go heavy on the wing, too. I have always done better on this pattern when it was tied as a dropper fly. Sizes 6, 8, and 10 will be useful.

White Wing Coachman and Royal Coachman. These all-time favorites are valuable night flies. Golden pheasant tail, peacock body (red sash, in the case of the Royal), white duck wing, and brown hackle. Use the fullest, fluffiest peacock herl you can find. As with the Cahill, I like to use these flies as droppers and make them tickle the surface. If rainbows frequent your water, they will usually hit this fly more readily than the browns.

Fiery Brown. This salmon pattern has worked well on brown trout. For night work, a good modification of this fly consists of a bronze turkey wing, red-brown hackle, and body spun from brown, yellow, and red mohair. The addition of a gold tip adds a spot of flash. The body is the tricky part of this fly. It should favor the red more than the brown. The touch of yellow makes the body's appearance a bit more vibrant. Best sizes will be 4 and 6.

Quill Gordon. Believe it or not, this somber fly that occupies such an important place in the world of dry-fly fishing is also a productive night fly. You tie it just as you would for daytime fishing, though the quill body causes some problems on the larger hooks. This fly works well for me in size 8 and even as large as 6.

Governor. This is the king of the night flies. If I had to be content to fish with one large wet forever, this would certainly be the pattern I'd choose. Dark brown turkey wing, fat, juicy peacock-herl body, red-brown hackle (fully tied — use at least two hackles), and bright-red tip. To make this body appear even fatter, wrap on some green wool underneath the herl to "flesh out" the fly. This is an especially good idea if you can't obtain good-quality herl. This fly is useful in all sizes from 12 through 2.

Gray Hackle. An easy fly to tie. It's nothing more than a herl body and two grizzly hackles wound on at the eye of the hook. The different bodies turn it into different flies. I like the yellow-wool body wound with gold tinsel and the red-floss body wound with silver tinsel. They are still Gray Hackles. Sizes 6 and 8 will be the best sizes.

Greenwell's Glory. Another old British pattern that will work well on some nights. Gray duck wing, olive-green floss body ribbed with gold tinsel, and coch-y-bodhu hackle. I once had some of these made by an obscure tier, and they had bodies of a delightful shade of greenish-brown dubbing. It may have been dyed seal fur. They caught fish, too!

Grizzly King. This is another green-bodied fly that has worked well for me. Some night fishermen like it better than the Professor. The barred gray mallard wing should be full and long. The hackle is grizzly, and the body a bright-green floss ribbed with silver tinsel. The serious night fisherman should carry Grizzly Kings in a good selection of sizes. Number 6s should prove to be the best, though I have successfully used this fly as large as number 2. It is a surprisingly good day-fly in the smaller sizes. I have made several good catches on badly pounded brown-trout streams, using a pair of size-14 Grizzly Kings fished wet.

Hardy's Favorite. The usual dressing for this pattern calls for a brown hackle, gray turkey wing, and body of scarlet floss ribbed with peacock herl. This pattern will catch trout at night, but the herl rib will soon be chewed off or cast off. I much prefer to tie a full peacock-herl body and then rib it with the scarlet floss. This is a much more durable arrangement. Brown English-partridge hackle is my choice for legs. In fact, the old British tackle catalogues listed the fly this way, and I think it makes a better-looking pattern. Sizes 4 and 6 will be best.

King of the Waters. Another nearly forgotten pattern that produces at night. Mallard wing, scarlet-floss body ribbed with silver tinsel, and brown hackle tied palmer fashion. This is a buggy-looking fly that I usually use as a dropper. It just seems to catch more fish in the number-two position. Sizes 6 and 8.

Leadwing Coachman and Red Ant. For all practical purposes, these two flies can fill the same compartment in the fly box. They are alike except for the body. The Coachman has an all-peacock-herl body, and the Ant has a red-floss body with herl butt. Slate duck wing and brown hackle. Gold tag or golden-pheasant-tippet tail, or both.

Lord Baltimore. A good black fly. Black duck wing, black hackle, and orange-floss body ribbed with black floss and sporting a black tail. I add a gold rib to the original dressing because it appeals to me. (I think the touch of gold also makes the fly more fishy-looking.) Number-8 light-wire salmon hooks work fine for this fly. In fact, light-wire salmon hooks are excellent night-fly steel. The looped eyes make up smoothly, and the points are usually sharper than those of bronzed hooks because the barbs, particularly on the Hardy salmon hook, are not nearly so coarse and can be set easily in a fish's mouth.

Montreal. Here is another of the popular Canadian brook-trout patterns that has made some history as a night fly, particularly for browns. I like the regular Montreal, which consists of claret body wound with silver-tinsel ribbing, claret hackle, and brown mottled turkey wing. The all-silver body is a good variation. Some like it better than the Silver Doctor.

Parmachene Belle. Another famous northern fly that ordinarily would startle a sophisticated brown. It has done well on certain nights, and in some fly boxes takes the place of the Royal Coachman. There must be a hundred dressings, but the one I like has a white wing with red stripes, mixed white and red hackle, and a yellow floss body ribbed with wide gold tinsel. Tail is mixed red and white hackle wisps. I almost always used this fly in size 8 and tie it on as a dropper. The flies that have some white in their make-up seem to work best in the dropper position.

Professor. Here is another of the great night flies. It's difficult to account for its success. It's not an unusual fly, but its reliability through the years makes it a must. Gray mallard wing, yellow floss body with gold rib, brown hackle, and red-hackle tail. Sizes 10 through 4 will be useful. Remember to tie it full. Use two or three hackles. Some tiers like it better with a brown mallard wing instead of the barred gray. The trout don't appear to make any distinction.

Queen of the Waters. There are times when an orange-bodied fly will be just what the trout want. The Queen is a good one and has a fuzzy appearance that I like. Brown hackle, tied palmer fashion, barred mallard wing, orange floss or dubbing body with a gold rib. You can add a golden-pheasant-tip tail if you like, though I don't think it matters much. This fly also works best as a dropper.

Silver Doctor. Another of the great ones. This fly has been tied so many ways that anyone could argue about what is standard. The important ingredients are red wool tag, silver body (flat silver tinsel ribbed with embossed silver tinsel), turkey or brown mallard wing, and bright-blue hackle faced with guinea. The addition of blue, scarlet, and green strips on both sides of the wing adds to the fly's beauty but is probably unnecessary for the fish. In my opinion, this is the handsomest fly that was ever created and, fortunately, it also catches trout. It is a pattern to show off the tier's skill and is guaranteed to dress up anyone's fly box. Sizes 6 and 8 are best.

Dozens of other patterns have been used to good effect by night flyers across the country. There are many local favorites that I have never heard of. I have seen good catches made on flies of practically every description, many of which will never be listed in any reference book of fly patterns. The Letort Black Cricket is a good example of a fine local favorite. Ed Shenk of Carlisle, Pennsylvania, who originated the Black Cricket, says that this is how he came to create it.

"In the late summer of 1959, the Letort Hopper was the 'fly' on our limestone waters. There were so many Letort Hoppers dancing around that some of the larger surface-feeding browns were becoming immune to it. One fish in particular would inspect the hopper but just wouldn't inhale it. I sat and pondered the situation and idly watched a big cricket hopping about at my feet. 'Why not a Letort Cricket?' I reasoned. I used the same tying style as for the hopper, except all ingredients were black. Next morning I took the above-mentioned fish on the first cast — a three-and-a-half-pound hook-jawed brown.

"Here's how to tie it. Hook should be 2X or 3X long, sizes 6 and 8 for night fishing, 12 to 18 for daytime. Body of dubbed black fur, wrapped medium thick. Wing of black goose quill tied flat over body extending beyond bend of hook. Hackle and head of black deer hair tied muddler style, head trimmed cylindrical instead of rounded like the Muddler."

Mrs Phillips' Yellow Dun, spoken of earlier, was another great night fly with only a local reputation. The Heather Moth and Theodore Gordon's Bumble Puppy — yes, dry-fly introverts, Gordon fished at night, too! — were others. The message here is simple: Experiment. There is still much to be learned about night fishing, and the development of fly patterns is one of the most fascinating aspects of it. At times, the patterns that work best suggest something natural. On other occasions, the bizarre will outfish the representational by a wide margin. And what great fun it is to try to figure out why.

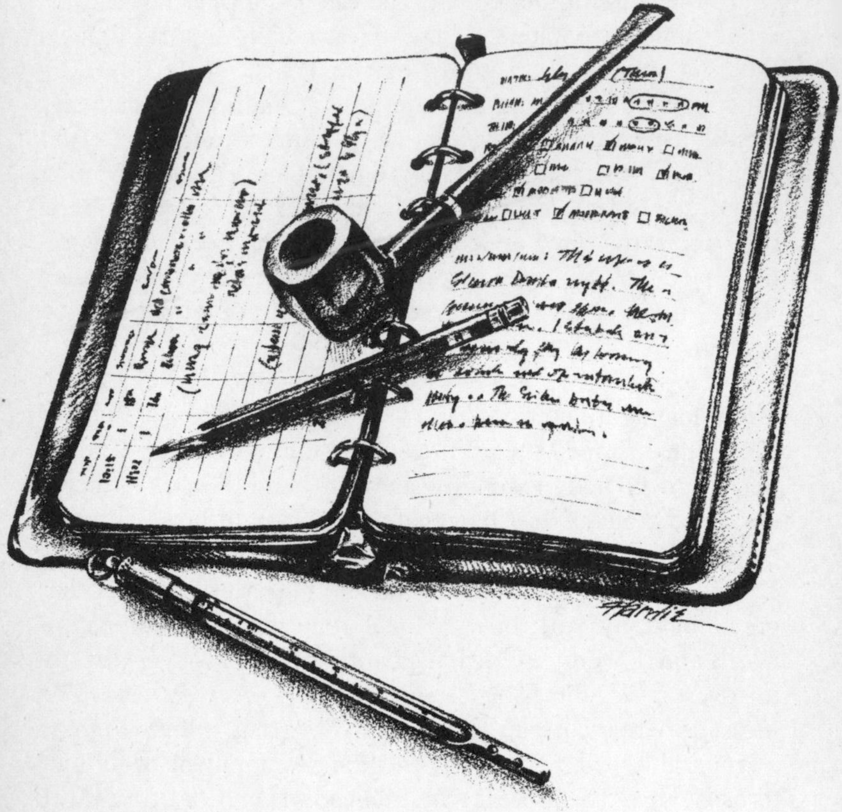

A DIARY OF SORTS

The following is not a chronological record of one particular year but rather a composite diary of the outstanding (and some not so outstanding) nights that I have enjoyed during my tenure as a night fly fisherman. As in all fishing, some nights are totally fishless. These nights can be just as rewarding to the thoughtful angler as the adventures that include a two-footer. The fruitless nights make the victories that much sweeter as they are recalled.

May 18. This was a bit early for good night fishing, but the fish were still in a feeding mood long after the sun had set. The air temperature had passed the eighty-degree mark by noon, and a splendid hatch of March Browns had brought some really big trout to the surface. The Oswayo was the target stream that evening, and I had had a measure of success with a number-12 Adams during the evening rise. It wasn't altogether an evening rise, since the fish had been feeding off and on all afternoon, or so another fisherman told me. There would be no moon until at least midnight, and the occasional slurp of a good trout gave me the itch to tie on a string of big wets and have a go at it.

A number-6 Governor was tied on the end and a number-8

Queen of Waters made up the dropper. I cast about five feet upstream from the last substantial rise ring and jiggled the flies twice to make them sink. On the second jiggle a splash and a sharp thud had me reflexively setting the hook. I always strike hard on the first strike of the season, so I really gave that fish the iron. As soon as I did, he headed upstream with amazing speed.

He didn't jump but chose to make his stand in midstream. After another run and much hard tugging, I was convinced that I had really hung myself a dandy. I was putting a lot of pressure on that fish. He was holding up better than any trout I had ever hooked in Pennsylvania waters. He was either the biggest thing in the river or else I had him foul-hooked. I was right on both counts. The fish was tiring, and though I seldom turn on a flashlight when night fishing, I now reached for my two-cell light and peered down over the two-foot gravel bank to which the fish had led me. I'm an excitable fisherman at best, but when I saw that great spotted trout I nearly dropped the rod. He was a monster — as long as my arm, and with a hooked beak that looked like a dog salmon's, and there was my number-6 Governor impaled lightly in his back, just behind the gills.

How I happened to hook him in that part of his anatomy I can only speculate, but I could easily see that the thin slip of skin was about to give way if I didn't do something in a hurry. I couldn't possibly lift him up over the bank, and to lead him downstream to the shallows in an attempt to beach him would probably be a mistake. The fish was floating there about six inches under the surface, obviously tired. Perhaps if I were very careful, I could reach down and lift him out by hand. I'm six foot two and have a pretty good reach, but this time I was overextending it. A small part of the bank I was kneeling on began to crumble, and suddenly I was very wet. The water was only about three feet deep. As I stumbled to my feet, I instinctively lifted the rod and hoped that the fish would still be there. He wasn't. I heard later that year that a huge trout had been taken from the same pool by a local farmer with a great reputation as a minnow fisherman. The fish was reported to have weighed nine pounds.

After hearing of the big fish, I decided that the minnow-caught fish was indeed my lost brown trout and wrote that particular trophy off as no longer available. Had it not been caught, I would have pursued that specimen on other nights, since large brown trout in fresh water streams don't move about all that much, especially fish that become night feeders. Tenacity pays off when fishing for nocturnal brown trout. The best of the night fishermen know this and that's why they can be spotted fishing in the same locations night after night until they catch a particular fish or decide someone else has.

The pool in question was only a "fair" night-fly location, but it was beautifully laid out for floating dry flies, and the silty bottom held a multitude of Green Drake nymphs. Whenever it was Green Drake time, I usually fished it during the best evenings. About two years after losing the big trout, I was there again, casting to a rise that had all the earmarks of being made by a big fish. When a natural drake would float over the fish's feeding location, it would vanish in a swirl that made me feel my four-pound tippet was very inadequate for the task at hand. The water was still and quite clear, and any leader diameter thicker than 3X would most likely be rejected. Getting into a good casting location required that I wade into the pool until the water level was precisely at the top of my boots.

At that time, my most productive fly during the Green Drake hatch was a size-10 variation of the Light Cahill that featured mint-green deer-hair wings. I tied on the best one I had, checked the hook point, applied a dab of mucilin, and wished it well. The first cast floated over the fish in a good drag-free attitude, but I was stymied by a natural that landed less than two inches from my fly. The big trout rose and sucked in the real dun beside my fake. The disturbance on the water was enough to increase my heartbeat, and so was the top half of the tail that appeared as the trout resumed its watching place. The part of the tail I could see was as big as my hand. I have a very large hand!

The big fish didn't rise for many Green Drakes — one every ten minutes or so, and he didn't rise for my imitation. But since it was the first week in June, and the night-fly season, I decided to stay on this big trout's case and rig up with a pair of large wets and a heavier tippet. The Green Drakes made my fly choice easy. The point fly would be a size-4 Light Cahill, tied fat and full, and the dropper a Grizzly King, its green floss body complete with silver rib.

I moved into a spot about thirty feet above where I had last seen the huge brown rise; from there I could attempt to float the duo of wets across his position in a dead drift. After a final tug on all the knots proved that my terminal tackle seemed ready for the job, I delivered the first cast with the big flies.

The flies had drifted for no more than six feet when I gave the line a short pull to straighten the leader. The flies probably moved an inch or so — and that must have triggered the attack. The rod tip slapped the water as the big brown gulped the fly. I struck hard, and as the hook found its mark the fish tore upstream.

The trout never jumped but chose to hang in the center of the pool and slug it out by pushing his nose into the bottom. I kept heavy pressure on him, knowing that the eight-pound tippet could handle it. After about five minutes of serious tug-of-war, the fish slowly came to the top, and in the dim light I saw a hint of white belly. Seeing that long band of white pushed my heart against my wading vest. This was a big fish! As big or bigger than the foul-hooked one of two years ago. As I mentally weighed and measured the brown he decided to make a last-ditch race for a tangled pile of brush on my side of the creek. This final surge of power convinced me that this was the largest brown I had ever hooked.

The bend in the rod was considerable. I thought I'd checked the escape run, but no such luck. The dropper fly locked onto a sunken limb in the brush pile and the rod tip went straight. But the fish was still on, hooked on the point fly. It was held fast, though, by the dropper. There was still hope. I quickly splashed to the trouble spot and, with an overwhelming sense of dejavu, snapped on the flashlight.

The fish was two feet under water and appeared to be spent. I gave no thought to releasing this monster. It was a "bragging" fish, and I wanted it. I'd figure out how to release the dropper fly after I had my fingers safely locked in the big trout's gills. Easing my right hand into the water for the killing grab, my jaw suddenly dropped. There on the back of the fish's head was a well-healed, gray scar. Did it mark the spot where the trout had once been hooked? Could this have been the trophy I lost two years ago?

Three inches from victory, my fingers closed on nothing as the brown made a final surge and the fly fell free from its jaw. I lunged . . . but it was too late. The fish, now six feet away, slowly fanned its tail and eased into the deep water. In the beam of the light I could plainly see that old scar until it was no more, until the huge shape was swallowed by the black water.

Of course, it's possible that the second encounter wasn't with the same fish I lost two years previously. Productive pools or good feeding positions are frequently taken over by other big fish — all experienced trout fishermen know this. But the circumstances were convincing. As the years passed I became more confident that it was indeed the same fish, and the second act of "Me and the Monster" had me convinced that this fish was well in excess of 12 pounds.

May 25. This was to be another good night for the Governor. I suppose this pattern must be my favorite. Pinney and the other Goodsell Hole regulars liked it slightly better than the Hardy's Favorite and usually tied one on as a dropper — they invariably did early in the season. I followed their advice. This evening I had not one but two Governors on my leader. I am not certain just how this came about, but so armed I hit the Goodsell Hole that night with such killing success that, in recalling it, I'm not a bit ashamed. It seemed to be one of those nights when a well-cast Argyle sock would have caught a trout. I must have taken at least fifteen fish, a twenty-two-incher the best and one of about fourteen inches the smallest. Earl Brown was there that night and so was Herman Grennels. Mr. Grennels always fished with minnows, and I don't think he caught more than one fish all night long. Brownie was fishing flies, and after my fifth or sixth fish he called across the water to ask what in the world I was using. I confessed it was the Governor, and he promptly tied one on. Just as promptly he was into a fish and proceeded to catch several more. I don't recall what patterns he had on before he changed flies, but, whatever they were, they hadn't been working. Looking back, I wish I hadn't been so greedy and had tried some other patterns, to test the trouts' selectivity. Perhaps they would have taken any fly with a peacock-herl body, and then again, perhaps not. At any rate, the Governor is a dandy, and I would not be caught without several in sizes 2 through 14.

May 28. Big Green Drakes on the water tonight. Not too many of them but enough to bring the big trout to the surface. Caught two twelve-inchers on a number-10 Light Cahill before dark but could not interest the bigger fish in a dry offering. Had several swirls behind the fly but nothing more positive. The heavy slurps continued after complete darkness had settled, so I tied on the big wets. My cast consisted of a number-6 Rube Wood and a number-8 Professor, two flies that had proved their worth on previous encounters with *E. guttulata*. On the second cast caught one small stocked rainbow that almost had to unhinge his mouth to latch onto the big Rube Wood. Caught two chubs and tossed them to Jack Dorfeld's cat, who was also a steady visitor to the Goodsell Hole. Large fish were still surfacing, so I changed flies, replacing the Rube Wood with a Silver Doctor. Still nothing. The moon came up, and as though a switch had been thrown, the trout stopped rising and activity came to a halt.

May 29. On the Allegheny about a mile upstream from Roulette. Rozell Stidd, the local game protector, was my fishing partner that night. Green Drakes on the water again but more of them. A bit early for so many of these big flies. The air was full of them, and big trout were actually making waves on the cemetery pool. It sounded like a bunch of hogs lapping up skim milk, which is a unique sound. I know, because an uncle of mine kept hogs and fed them skim milk.

Rozy and I took several nice fish on number-10 dry Light Cahills, and he lost one that might have gone two feet. I was watching when the trout sucked his fly under, and the resulting swirl looked like someone had tossed a Shetland pony into the river. After one run and one jump, the fish came unglued. Rozy did too, and it took over a half hour for him to regain his composure. Fortunately, he recovered soon enough to partly make up for his loss, after tying on a big number-4 Grizzly King. I took four rather smallish fish that night (on the big wets), while he racked up a half dozen very respectable browns on the big gray fly. It had never occurred to me that a trout might mistake the G.K. for a submerged Green Drake, but they sure did that night and, always to my surprise, continue to do so from time to time.

Before this experience I had never seriously considered the Grizzly King a night fly. I've used it often since that night. It works particularly well when there is a fall of measuring worms. Size 8 is probably best, although Rozy liked his Grizzly Kings to be decidedly large.

(It is interesting to note that Rozy Stidd liked to fish a pair of large wets across and upstream. His standard method was to make a long cast upstream and wait a considerable period for his flies to sink. Then he would retrieve his cast with a slow, deliberate hand-over-hand movement, "feeling" the way along the bottom. This is not orthodox night-fishing technique, but it worked well for him, and, at times, has worked for me. When across and downstream casts are not producing well, the upstream cast should be given a chance.)

June 4. Tom Leete and I fished the tail end of the flood-control channel on this night. This extremely difficult spot contained some really superselective trout that had lost all fear of humans. Like all big trout in hard-fished locations, these were most difficult creatures to entice. Leete got lucky before dark and took an eighteen-inch rainbow that weighed a full three pounds. The fish had been cruising around in the concrete channel, sucking in some sort of minutiae and making a general nuisance of himself, when Tom's muskrat nymph got in his line of attack. Tom made a wooden cutout of this fish, and it still hangs in his den. He has caught many fish that were much bigger but never another one so hefty for its length. I mention this to disprove the myth that trout in freestone streams cannot be well fed. It is often said that, inch for inch, limestone-water fish will outweigh all others because of their longer growing season and more plentiful food supply. This may be so generally, but there are many freestone streams like the Allegheny that have long stretches of mud bottom. Although not picture-book waters, such streams produce tons of fish food.

On this particular night we couldn't do much with the big night flies during the early part of the session. Several big fish were cruising and swirling, but we couldn't entice them to more than a half-hearted pass or two. Because I am an incurably experimental fly tier, I usually have some oddballs in my fly book. A few weeks before, a friend had given me some blue gantron floss, and after wondering for a while what it might be good for, I tied up some size-8 Blue Bottle wets. The blue floss was really bright. You could almost see it glow in the dark. I announced to Tom that I was going to tie on a new secret pattern and catch a big trout. By skittering the Blue Bottle across the surface, I did exactly that. In fact, I caught four very good fish. It must have been a fluke because I have since caught nothing on that fly. (After that, we always referred to any night when the trout were not receptive to our usual offerings as "a Blue Bottle sort of night.")

June 9. For many years after nylon became the standard material for leaders, Pinney still preferred the traditional gut. Before starting a night's fishing he would frequently sit down on a driftwood bench at the tail end of the Goodsell Hole and toss out his leader to soak. One night Pinney sat soaking his leader, looking to all appearances like a man who was still-fishing. I was on the opposite bank. The night wasn't completely dark yet but rather in an advanced stage of twilight. Suddenly I heard a mighty splash from his side of the river.

"What is it?" I called across.

"Trout," was the brief reply. "About two feet long."

"How do you know how big it is?"

"Because it's right here on the bank." And so it was.

Only the leader and about two feet of line had been hanging from the rod tip, and apparently the big fish had seen the fly just as Pinney started to lift it to make his first cast of the evening. He had hooked the trout and skidded it onto the bank all in one motion. I told him that I knew he always fought his fish hard but that this was ridiculous. He admitted that he had never landed a big trout so fast before.

Incidentally, an autopsy showed that this trout's stomach was completely empty. The fish was not in poor condition, for it weighed nearly five pounds. The unexpected is commonplace when fishing after dark.

June 12. The first fork of the Sinnemahoning below the little town of Costello, Pennsylvania, is a beautiful piece of water. It's not nearly as rich in food as some of the other freestone streams, but it has always been a good night stream.

I was there with my wife this evening, and though we didn't see much surface activity to floating insects, there was a lot of splashing and swirling going on in the tail of the long, flat pool just below the Costello bridge. The "V" wakes indicated big trout. To me, the situation called for a Silver Doctor. A streamer would have been a more conventional choice, but I have never had much luck with the long flies on big browns after dark. The Silver Doctor or the Montreal Silver have always been better producers for me when big trout were working on minnows at night.

I tied a size-6 Silver Doctor on the end and a Hare's Ear on the dropper. As soon as it became fully dark, I tossed the pair out into the slick tail water and immediately had a good, solid strike. I knew instantly that the strike was on the dropper because the trout came part way out of the water to grab it. It felt like a fifteen- or sixteen-incher, and I was delighted to perform so quickly and heroically in front of my new bride. The fish was racing upstream into deeper water when suddenly there came another powerful jerk on the rod, and a helluva commotion on the surface seemed to indicate that a second, much bigger fish was hooked. Sylvia was standing where she could catch what light was still reflecting off the water. She shouted that there were two fish out there, and so there were. A second trout, much bigger than the first, had seized the Silver Doctor as it was being dragged through the deeper water. The bigger fish was pulling the smaller one, and he soon wore himself out.

I was soon leading two very badly tired-out trout as best I could to the shallow water at the lip of the pool. I hoped to skid them gently onto the bank. The fish on the dropper was coming along nicely, and the tail and dorsal fin of the larger fish was beginning to make an appearance. He was a dandy! At least twenty inches. Suddenly his belly touched the gravel bottom and he gave a mighty flop and was off. The sudden change in tension caused the fly to drop out of the smaller trout's mouth, and there were two good trout floundering in shallow water, neither one attached to anything. Sylvia and I made a rush to grab them, ran into each other, and slipped and sprawled on our bellies in six inches of water. Both fish escaped. . . . For a silent moment we lay in the water, not speaking. The humor of the situation hit us at the same instant, and we started to laugh. It was a great evening.

June 15. Pinney and I were alone at Goodsell's this night. For some reason, he wasn't doing his usual good job of casting. The trouble was diagnosed as a worn tip-top on his glass rod, which was almost new. He didn't care much for glass rods, and grumbling about the inferior quality of the fittings used on them, he reeled up and walked home to get another rod. He was only gone for forty-five minutes, but what a mistake he made. He hadn't been gone more than five minutes when the fish went on a rampage.

In rapid succession, I caught five good trout of up to eighteen inches and had over a dozen strikes. The fish were ripping and tearing across the water, hitting any pattern that I tossed out. Pinney returned just in time to catch a couple before the action stopped, as quickly as it had begun. I mean things went dead!

We snapped on our flashlights to see if a hatch was present. There was none. A mystery. Several days later we compared notes with Ray Goodrich, who had been fishing a half mile downstream at the old Chestnut Street bridge. He reported the same experience: a forty-five-minute feeding rampage and then nothing. It seemed as though every trout in the river had briefly gone crazy. A sudden nighttime hatch? A rapid change in barometer? Some peculiar heavenly phenomenon?

At times, the same sort of thing happens when one is dry-fly fishing or bait fishing. Some strange "X factor" seems to set off the feeding urge. It follows that something must be there for the trout to feed on. Or does it? I killed two of the five fish I caught that evening, and a midnight autopsy showed that these fish were absolutely empty, save for a few grains of gravel. This empty-stomach business at night is baffling. Big night-caught trout are so often empty that it seems to prove that reasons other than hunger will move a good trout into striking. This appears to increasingly be the case as the season progresses.

June 18. At the Goodsell again. Couldn't beg a strike. Fish were slurping Pale Evening Dun spinners like kids eating peanuts. They began to feed just before dark and continued into the night. Changed flies a dozen times. Tried big ones, small ones, drys and nymphs, but couldn't interest anything. Fog appeared about 10:30, so I went home. The old-timers always declared that the fish stopped feeding when the fog started to rise, and on this night they were right. Heard later that Boney Shaw caught two big browns and a rainbow on crayfish at about two in the morning.

June 25. This had to be the night. There was a beautiful sunset (always a good sign) and a medium-size hatch of pink-bodied mayflies that Tom Leete thought were *Potamanthus distinctus*. It was a beautiful fly, and the trout began to come for them an hour before darkness. It seemed sensible to tie on a size-16 Tups, and it was. Several small fish were rising in the "whirlpool" current in the center of Goodsell's, and if your fly would float for more than twelve inches without dragging, a fish would hit it. No big fish were showing themselves yet. I tied on a pair of the big wets and was promptly fast to a fair fish. It proved to be a rainbow of about twelve inches. Another followed, and another, and another, and — Whoa, now! What in the world was happening? On the opposite side of the creek another fisherman, a stranger to me, was having the same luck. He was fishing flies, too, and was hauling out one twelve-inch rainbow after another. It was fast fishing, to be sure, but the Allegheny just didn't have that many rainbows in it, not this late after spring stocking. It was like fishing in a hatchery, and that was almost the case.

The puzzle was solved the next day when it was reported that Fred Eckert's Rainbow Paradise, a fee-fishing project about seven miles upstream, had lost a whole pond full of two-year-old rainbows while repairs were being made on a connecting pond race. The fish, used to still water, had just drifted downstream in a pod and collected in the Goodsell Hole. They were not there the next day. They must have moved on. The stranger — I found out he was from New Jersey — was back for the next four nights but didn't catch a fish. I didn't have the heart to tell him what had happened.

June 28. Pinney announced that he had seen a tremendous trout in the Belknap Hole, which was about two hundred yards downstream from Goodsell's. The sun had been hitting the water just right, and he swore the fish was thirty inches. "Spots as big as a nickel," Pinney declared. He reported that the trout was just fanning in the lip of the pool and doing nothing in particular. Since big fish were Bob's game, I know he would fish for that trout after darkness had settled in. He did, and he caught it. It was not thirty inches long, but it was a full twenty-seven and weighed better than six pounds — a very respectable brown trout in any water. What he caught it on was the shocker.

The trout had begun to chase minnows (or something) just at dusk, so Pinney tied on his usual string of three proven producers — the Silver Doctor, the Hardy's Favorite, and the Professor. Nothing. He changed flies several times, but still to no effect. The fish was still feeding, so he kept on trying. On a pure hunch (or perhaps out of desperation), he tied on the biggest fly in his box. It was a number-2/0 Fiery Brown, a whole handful of feathers. He showed me the fly — it looked as big as a hummingbird. The first cast made the trout swirl behind it, and the second cast had him, right through the snout. That fly was a 2/0, mind you, not a conventional number 2. I have taken trout on big flies, but never on one that big.

June 30. Fished a private pond this evening. It was known to contain some big brookies, but they were tough to catch. Before dark, caught one about a foot long on a small wet fly (I think it was an Orange Fish Hawk). After dark, the moon was bright and full and, wonder of wonders, the trout were still feeding. Changed flies many times, but couldn't hit on the right combination. Tied on a big fluffy cream bivisible and skittered it across the surface. A fat fourteen-incher attached himself. Three more of the same size followed, and then a whopper took the fly off clean. Tied on another fly, but apparently the commotion had put the fish down. It was a small pond, so I wasn't surprised that they quit. This particular night wouldn't have been especially memorable had it not been for the bright moon. It is the only bright night I can recall when trout hit well. I've wondered if they would have risen to the dry fly if they had been brown trout.

July 4. The Roulette Fire Department was putting on a fireworks display, and from the Reed Run bridge an occasional rocket blast could be seen, and then, a second later, heard. I'm sure the trout weren't aware of the celebration; they reacted in a most unpatriotic manner. Just before dark a hatch of big *Ephemera varias* appeared on the surface, and the trout were having a field day with them. I caught two on a big Light Cahill before the fireworks started. Then the action stopped. My usual number-6 wets were not producing. I went to a smaller size, and that seemed to do the trick. Number 10s were the size wanted, and a Wickham's Fancy at the number-two position on the leader was just the ticket.

There seemed to be a huge school of fish right where the cool fan of water from Reed Run met the Allegheny, and the trout were clustered in a tight little pod just below a rather fast falling riffle. I reasoned that the dropper was dancing in the current at just the right attitude to entice them. Didn't catch anything really big, but all of the trout hit hard in the faster water and gave a good account of themselves. The fish were mostly twelve-inchers, with few of them going over that. Several were well-colored rainbows. This was unusual, as no rainbows had been stocked in the river since April 10. They could have come down Reed Run, but the fish usually stocked in that brook are much smaller. (Note: I have since changed my mind about rainbows always moving downstream after being stocked. There appears to be a strain of rainbows that do not instinctively migrate to the ocean. Unfortunately, the rainbows raised by most hatcheries are of such mixed ancestry that heaven only knows whether we can legitimately call them rainbows. They have become ugly, big-headed freaks that bear little resemblance to the broad-chested, small-headed, streamlined fish originally found in the Pacific drainage system. As stream fodder, they serve our purposes reasonably well. They are easy to raise in hatcheries, and, through manipulation of individual fish, biologists have created strains that become ripe at all times of the fall and spring, thus providing stockable fish for all seasons.)

July 5. Water was very low in the Sinnemahoning, and water temperature at the stream's edge was nearly seventy. There was no surface activity on insects, but at dusk some large swirls commenced to appear at the lip of the long Costello Hole. One very good fish took up a feeding position right at the edge of the fast water and after each foray returned to the same spot. I could easily see his dorsal fin and a tip of his tail as he fanned there. The water for ten feet in front of him was no more than eight inches deep, so there were two good reasons why drifting a night fly to him would be difficult. He was stationed beside a partially submerged bush that would probably foul my flies and spook him if he didn't take, and the shallow water made a long drift almost impossible to make without snagging the flies on the bottom.

After fifteen minutes of careful thought I came upon a solution. Since I felt certain this trout would take a big wet, the problem was how to gently float a slightly submerged number-8 Silver Doctor to him. The tip end of my fly line was rather chewed up, and I knew it would not float well, so I cut off about fifteen feet of it, thus getting into a good piece of coating. I shortened the leader to three feet and tied on a single Silver Doctor. The idea, of course, was to keep the fly from sinking too quickly before it got to the fish. The cast was made about ten feet in front of him and, thank goodness, the fish didn't start. I could see the white fly line drifting toward the fish. When the fly was about ten inches in front of his snout (or so I guess), I gave the rod tip a gentle twitch. Swirl-jerk-strike!

Instead of turning quickly to the right and tangling up the little bush, this brown elected to plow straight ahead into the center of the pool and slug it out. He jumped once at the end of his run and then resigned himself to five minutes of boring for the bottom. The short leader and a good corner-of-the-mouth hold had him on the losing end of the tussle. He weighed five and a quarter pounds. I was most pleased with myself for catching that particular fish.

July 10. The water was very low in the Prouty Run, and the brooks and browns were ultraskittish. I managed to take a couple before dark on a Royal Coachman Bivisible and ended up at the big beaver dam that used to be situated at the foot of Wild Boy Road. All the trout for a mile of stream must have been congregated at that dam, for as darkness fell the pool was a solid mass of rises. The insects on the water were truly minute. Thousands of them could be put into a circle the size of a penny, so it seemed hopeless to attempt to imitate them. I tried wets and nymphs down to 24s, but nothing happened. Then I went through the usual night fly fisherman's bag of tricks, starting out with a pair of number-8 wets, followed by 6s, then 10s, then 12s.

A trip back to the car to find a lighter leader also produced a box of Stewart Spiders that Tom Lette had given me. These were nothing more than thread bodies with soft bird hackles — no wings. They were mostly tied on 16 and 18 hooks and looked entirely too small for night use. Nevertheless, I tied on a pair after changing to a 4X tippet. For an hour I hooked brookie after brookie on those little spiders.

It was some of the fastest fishing I have ever enjoyed. The trout were not large, so I was dragging them in without too much finesse. Klunk! Suddenly I was fastened to something a bit larger. I thought for a second I had hooked a beaver, since I had done just that at this dam a year before. This fish was not to be hauled out unceremoniously. It made a solid run and stripped out a good forty feet of line. Since beaver dam bottoms are loaded with all sorts of obstacles, I gave myself little chance of landing that fish, but luck won out. After a bit of chugging on the bottom, he allowed himself to be led to the breastwork of the dam, where I managed to slip my hand under him. Sixteen inches of very fat brook trout was hooked solidly in the corner of the mouth. This was before my first trip to Canadian trout waters, so that fish was, at the time, the largest brook trout I had ever taken. It was a beautifully marked male. The autopsy I performed at home that night produced a baseball-size wad of minutiae. That fish must have been feeding all day long.

July 17. Pinney caught a bat this night. He had caught them before, and he detested them. The incident wouldn't have been worth mentioning were it not for the havoc it caused. Bats will frequently seize a night fly on the back cast and can usually be jiggled free. This one wouldn't come loose, and in the scuffle to dislodge it, a loop of line got wound around the stem of Bob's pipe, which happened to be in his mouth. In trying to free his pipe, he looped his line over his fishing-license button, which was on his hat. The cursing and muttering rose in a crescendo as he finally subdued the bat and stomped it to death, then discovered he had also been stomping his pipe into a dozen pieces, flattening his hat, and smashing his rod tip. He could not see the humor in the situation, but I didn't stop laughing for a week.

July 21. This was a Silver Doctor night. The Genesee River above the town of Genesee and just over the New York State line was the target stream, and the big browns were really on the rampage. I was not completely familiar with the pool I had decided to fish, so I started the evening off by losing a whole string of flies on a submerged "something" that seemed to dominate the center of the pool. (When the water dropped the following month, I discovered that the "something" was an entire automobile body. How it got in the center of the river, I have no idea.)

The snag was right at the end of the little web of current that marked the center of the pool. To send the night flies sweeping across the tail of the pool in an interesting manner one had to drop the cast right on top of the sunken hulk. About every fifth cast found me hung up on the damned thing, but every tenth cast produced a strike. And what strikes they were. The speed of the current swept the flies along so fast that the fish had to rise with a rush and seize them before they washed over the lip of the pool. Perhaps any fly with tinsel would have worked as well, but the Silver Doctor with all the gingerbread, including golden pheasant topping, was doing so well that I hesitated to experiment.

My first strike proved to be a husky sixteen-inch brown that had spots the size of a dime. He was a beautiful fish, with the big red adipose fin that used to be a characteristic of a larger Allegheny River trout. I caught and released four or five twelve- and thirteen-inchers, all on the Silver Doctor, and then I made a fantastic catch. A bullfrog that must have weighed two pounds swam into my line, and striking instinctively, I hooked him in the leg. I thought for a second that I had foul-hooked a trout, but the surging on the tip of the rod didn't spell fish. Night fishing is full of surprises, and as I fought the thing, I was trying guess what it was. I was thankful it wasn't a water snake (they always have a nasty disposition and must be killed if you want your fly back) as I slid the frog out onto the bank. I sent the frog on his way, a little wiser about Silver Doctors, and resumed fishing.

It was a great night. I released at least a dozen fish and gave two the last rites and laid them on the bank. One was a brown of nineteen inches and the other a rainbow of nearly eighteen inches. That rainbow was the only fish that did not hit the Silver Doctor. He went for a Mills Number One, the only white-hackled fly that I have ever taken fish on at night.

Many fly fishermen rate the rainbow as slightly less intelligent than the brown. I'm not sure how an I.Q. test should be applied to a fish, but it does seem to be a general truth that the smaller rainbows are especially active feeders and can often be fooled with unsophisticated angling methods. When they approach the fifteen-inch mark, though, they can be just as fussy as the browns in picking off surface insects. As a night fish, however, the rainbow is not the feeder that the brown is, at least not in eastern waters. This is particularly so during the latter part of the season. When daylight water temperatures begin to rise into the high sixties and lower seventies, the rainbow tends to become quite sluggish. During May and June, rainbows can be taken at night without too much difficulty. Any of the good brown trout flies will catch them, the brighter patterns being best of all. The Silver Doctor, Jock Scott, Professor, and Grizzly King are favorite rainbow patterns. As a general rule, rainbows like the flies to move through the water at a fast pace. The old standard wet-fly retrieve consisting of a sweep and jerk works fine for the rainbow. However, this method will seldom move a trophy brown at night.

Until not too long ago, fishing for trout came to an end in Pennsylvania on the last day of July. Therefore, for many years, my experiences after that date were limited to an occasional trip to unfamiliar waters. In recent years, a more enlightened group of lawmakers have extended the regular trout season until Labor Day, and in special waters until the end of October. As much as I prefer wet flies for night work, dry flies will frequently outfish them during the fall months. Just why this is so is not apparent to me, but a "worked" dry fly, one of the Wulffs or a large floppy fanwing, can drum up a big trout on almost any September trout stream. Here again, there is a similarity to Atlantic salmon fishing. The so-called fall run of Atlantics will come to a surface fly much more readily than will the spring and summer fish. The height of the water may be a factor, but other anglers of a scientific bent believe that there may possibly be a chemical change in the water that causes trout and salmon to alter their behavior. The dissolved-oxygen factor certainly changes, and quite probably the chemical makeup of the water also varies from season to season.

I have proved to my own satisfaction that trout and many other game fish respond to night fishing with large flies in most parts of the country, with the possible exception of the far North and the high-altitude country of the Rockies and the Sierras. The availability of night food is certainly a factor, and in those regions the insects that fish feed on are not too plentiful.

In streams that contain smallmouth bass, and many trout streams do, the scrappy smallmouth proves to be a good night taker. He will hit the large wets as readily as he will a sputtering Jitterbug, Flipper, or Tiny Torpedo. Largemouth bass, walleyes, and catfish are also good night feeders, and though the last two are mostly a bait-fishing proposition, they prove that many freshwater fish do a large percentage of their eating at night.

In saltwater, snook, striped bass, and weakfish are also good night takers. The best snook fishing I've ever experienced occurred one night beneath the Ten Cent Bridge in Stuart, Florida. Ten-pounders were coasting in schools just behind the shadow of the bridge, and a large saltwater streamer or flashy Mirrolure would usually coax one to strike. What a ball that was, trying to keep the fish from cutting off the line on the bridge abutments. It was an expensive evening in terms of tackle lost but was nevertheless one of the most exciting nights I've ever enjoyed.

AND IN CONCLUSION

Fishermen who write books must be ever watchful that they do not become too dogmatic. It is easy to slip in a few remarks that snidely suggest this or that fellow is to be pitied because he fishes in some certain way. I suppose that I, too, have occasionally been guilty of this. Now the sight of a single bubble marking the spot where a size twenty-two Jassid has floated but a moment before is a thrill of major proportions (the fact that the Jassid is attached to a 7X tippet tends to heighten the thrill). And the surge of a solid strike on a streamer fly, followed by the leap of a runaway rainbow, sets my heart pounding, too. And, yes, though I admit it reluctantly, the *chug, chug, chug* of a native brookie eating my grasshopper is also fun. As Arnold Gingrich pointed out in *The Well-Tempered Angler*, "any fishing is better than no fishing."

My only defense for being a night fisherman, if I must have a defense, is that in the region where I was brought up you had to fish at night. It was the thing that fly fishermen did, if they deserved the name, in northcentral Pennsylvania. The respected anglers of the region fished at night, and if you hoped to earn a place among them, night fishing was a required part of the curriculum.

The end of a book is, I'll admit, a curious place to insert a dedication, but I'd like to do just that. This book is devoted to the dozen or so master anglers that took a wetnosed kid into their fold and taught him all that they knew. Bob Pinney, Ray Goodrich, Glenn and Rathbone Shaw, Howard Smith, T.M. Dilloway, Earl Brown, Andy Carpenter, and Duke Chilson could all have written books about night fishing. In a way, they wrote this one. My fishing contemporaries also contributed to this offering in many ways. First, they went fishing with me. They helped me to try new patterns and new techniques and freely shared their information. You won't find their names on any list of angling greats, but in their local bailiwicks they are as good as this country has ever produced. I won't list the greats, the near-greats, the lesser-knowns, and the unknowns with whom I've fished, but one name must be mentioned.

Tom Leete, of Coudersport, Pennsylvania, was and still is my favorite fishing companion. We have shared the same pools a thousand times, and though we now live two hundred miles apart, we still manage to fish together a time or two every season. An amateur entomologist, a skilled outdoorsman, and a crack wet-fly fisherman, this man is a delight to be with, always. If there is a special heaven for fly fishermen, I hope that Tom and I will have the luck to draw the same beat.

And there you have it, my friends. I wish I could tell you more about night fishing for trout, but I'm still learning. If you haven't already tried tossing the feathers at night, I sincerely hope that this book has offered you an incentive. Catching trout at night, when other anglers are fast asleep or busy with mundane tasks, has a peculiar fascination. I know of no other facet of the fly-fishing game that is more thought provoking, more mysterious, or more exciting.